WEISS
MANFREDI
SURFACE
SUBSURFACE

WEISS
MAN
SURFA
SUBSU

WEISS/MANFREDI: SURFACE/SUBSURFACE
MICHAEL A. MANFREDI AND MARION WEISS
FOREWORD BY MOHSEN MOSTAFAVI
INTRODUCTION BY DAVID LEATHERBARROW
CONVERSATION WITH DETLEF MERTINS
PRINCETON ARCHITECTURAL PRESS, NEW YORK

NFREDI
ACE
RFACE

Published by
Princeton Architectural Press
37 East Seventh Street
New York, New York 10003

For a free catalog of books,
call 1.800.722.6657.
Visit our web site
at www.papress.com.

Publication of this book has been
supported by a grant from the School
of Design, University of Pennsylvania.

Editor: Jennifer Thompson
Designer: Michael Bierut
and Jennifer Kinon, Pentagram

Special thanks to: Nettie Aljian, Sara Bader,
Dorothy Ball, Nicola Bednarek, Janet
Behning, Becca Casbon, Penny (Yuen Pik)
Chu, Russell Fernandez, Pete Fitzpatrick,
Wendy Fuller, Jan Haux, Clare Jacobson,
John King, Nancy Eklund Later, Linda Lee,
Laurie Manfra, Katharine Myers, Lauren
Nelson Packard, Arnoud Verhaeghe,
Paul Wagner, Joseph Weston, and Deb
Wood of Princeton Architectural Press —
Kevin C. Lippert, publisher

Library of Congress
Cataloging-in-Publication Data

Manfredi, Michael A., 1953-
  Weiss/Manfredi: surface/subsurface /
Michael Manfredi, Marion Weiss;
foreword by Mohsen Mostafavi;
introduction by David Leatherbarrow.
    p. cm.
  ISBN-13: 978-1-56898-733-0 (alk. paper)
  ISBN-10: 1-56898-733-1 (alk. paper)
  1. Weiss/Manfredi Architects—Catalogs.
2. Architecture—United States—20th
century—Catalogs. 3. Architecture—
United States—21st century—Catalogs.
4. Architecture—Environmental aspects—
United States—Catalogs. I. Weiss, Marion,
1957- II. Title.
  NA737.W398A4 2008
  720.92'2-dc22

FOREWORD
GEOLOGICAL ARCHITECTURE, MOHSEN MOSTAFAVI

There is a certain guise of normalcy in the type of projects undertaken by Weiss/Manfredi. Like many other practices, they design buildings and urban projects, interiors, and furniture. At the same time, not just in terms of their interdisciplinary focus but also in the quality of their work, they aspire to and achieve a great deal more. In that sense they are a-typical, a rarity amongst contemporary American practices.

Those unfamiliar with the nuances of contemporary architecture may find it hard to appreciate the potential correlations between the organization of an architectural practice and its design thinking. If we were to survey American practices as a whole, we would see that innovation is found mainly among the larger firms, which have developed programmatic, technical, and typological specializations that are able to deliver complex buildings for an ever-increasing pool of international corporate clients.

It is much harder to name a sufficient number of excellent small and mid-size firms that consistently produce buildings of international significance. Why is this? One suspects the main culprit to be the very circumstances of architectural practice in the United States—the rules and regulations, the financial realities, the legal liabilities, and, perhaps most importantly, the nature of expectations. It is the expectations of the client, the statutory bodies, the users, and of course the general public that seem to leave the most memorable mark on the project. In this challenging context, Weiss/Manfredi have been drawn to competitions as a research vehicle, because they are, to a great extent, discipline-blind and free from preconceived administrative burdens. They have had the good fortune to win competitions, to work with enlightened clients, and to have the persistence to hold onto ideas that matter.

Engagement with the site in its broadest sense is one of the distinguishing features of the work of Weiss/Manfredi. In their projects the area under consideration is often much larger than the actual building site and more akin to the territory of forces that affect construction, which includes the infrastructure. Their commitment to architecture as an interdisciplinary practice emerges from this larger view of site. These two elements are of course related; the connection between infrastructure, landscape, and architecture is a subject of methodical research that necessitates collaboration with a wide spectrum of consultants, while the involvement of a diversity of interests and expertise produces its own broad agenda of topics across a range and scale of artifacts.

Weiss/Manfredi's far-ranging interest in design is exemplified by their Olympic Sculpture Park in Seattle, Washington, where they simultaneously worked on a piece of infrastructure, a new landscape, a work of architecture, and pieces of furniture (such as a resin-coated table for outdoor use). They refer to the notion of a "gradient of attention" as a way of teasing out the common thread that connects these artifacts across their respective disciplinary fields. This approach has resonances of what Aldo Rossi termed analogical thinking where, for example, the design of a coffee pot is thought to have parallels with the design of a building.

A defining characteristic of Weiss/Manfredi's work from the very start has been the interaction between architecture and landscape. Rather than follow the modernist tradition of envisioning architecture as pure objects in the landscape, they tend to prefer to fuse the two together—except in their case,

the landscape is just as artificial as the architecture that conjoins it. The external topography itself becomes a form of clearing—a gigantic landscape receptacle, or an outdoor room of sorts—that receives the building and in the process not only accommodates and shapes it but also is shaped by it. As a kind of "architecture in the expanded field," this mode of practice shares a lineage with recent strands of land art—a fact that is clearly discernable in the Museum of the Earth building, which constructs new topographies as much from the juxtaposition of the elements of the architecture as it does from the formation of the landscape.

At the Olympic Sculpture Park, the impact of the landscape extends to the broader category of infrastructure as well as to geology, hydrology, and man-made residues and remnants of the complex brownfield site. Weiss/Manfredi negotiate

and utilize these topics to the project's advantage, working in collaboration with various artists to provide the most appropriate setting for their work— an open and accessible public space. The users of the sculpture park are actors in a performance enabled by the sectional setting. Through their presence and their movements they uncover the pleasures of art and the city.

Weiss/Manfredi's interest in landscape architecture also extends to co-opting its methods as a form of material practice. Just as landscape architects always begin with a given site that has to be transformed, Weiss/Manfredi too unravel their projects from the given material. At the Olympic Sculpture Park this material includes the artworks, which directly influence the conceptual articulation of the park, and in turn shape their reception. An attentiveness to materials and their effects as a mechanism

for the formation of precepts—and eventually perhaps even concepts— is evident in their other projects, such as their design for The Barnard College Nexus in New York City.

This intellectual underpinning of Weiss/Manfredi's work is influenced by their commitment to the wider debates around architecture and education. The themes they address in their practice are explored in parallel with their studio teaching, yielding reciprocities—interdisciplinary, material-based, open-ended—that benefit both their practice and the academy.

Akin to the geology of a site, their approach to architecture is multilayered yet has its own specific density. Contemporary architecture needs more critical practices like Weiss/Manfredi.

INTRODUCTION
UNFORESEEN BEAUTY, DAVID LEATHERBARROW

Presented under the title Surface/Subsurface, the recent work of Marion Weiss and Michael Manfredi poses a question that is both difficult and important: how can architecture with such obvious visual beauty be understood to depend on conditions that are not essentially visual, conditions that exercise their influence without making a show of it, operating somewhere beneath, behind, or beyond the work's surfaces, conditions that constitute the work's sub-surface?

Initially, it would seem that concern for conditions of this kind is not new. At least since the time of the New Brutalism, possibly before, more than a few architects have seen fit to expose systems and elements that were hidden or covered over in earlier architectures, infrastructure at one scale or another. What had been unseen, because insignificant or unseemly, was put on display. Perhaps it was because construction in the post-World War II years had to make do with materials as found that architects began to insist on direct exposure, as if what had been taken for granted no longer could be. One suspects that the necessity of substructures was never doubted by earlier architects, only their role in the building's image. The school at Hunstanton in Norfok, England, by Alison and Peter Smithson is a good example of how elements that were once hidden were newly shown off—I'm thinking of the drain lines that hang down from the bathroom sinks and empty into a channel cut into the floor. Yet, the exposé of the building's working parts was not intended to be pictorial or scenographic. Reyner Banham described it as an architectural "ethic." Can the same be said for current work

that demonstrates a concern for the "operations" or "performance" of architectural elements? Is our concern also evidence of an ethical position?

Projects by the Smithsons and others who took up this stance are good precedents for contemporary architecture that seeks to acknowledge the significance of substructures, except for the fact that earlier designs failed to raise what has become the radical question posed by the recent interest in the building's underlying parts: How can a work's conceptual and physical substrate be acknowledged in the project without rendering it as another surface, thereby annulling its role as an implicit conditioning power? The projects by Marion Weiss and Michael Manfredi not only face this question directly but also offer some compelling answers.

In architectural experience the building is what we see, what we see is the building. No statement could be more obvious. The work under consideration here, however, suggests that this premise is far from clear. First of all, no building rests in and of itself; each participates in its surroundings and is enmeshed in a milieu that is not of its own making but exists prior to construction. As given, this horizon allows for the derivation of the building's orientation, distances, and structure; not only through elaboration, extension, or cultivation alone but also through divergence. This framework is equally physical and practical; it could be called a topography of praxis. This topography is what allows the building to advance into visibility, for every figure depends on a ground, against which it appears. But such an appearance is

rarely adequate to the work, or to the topography, of which it is part; for in concrete experience buildings and landscapes only show aspects of themselves, inasmuch as they are always correlated to perceptual interests that vary over time. The fact that topography gives itself through movement—one step and view, followed by another—makes this principle obvious. What is seen at any moment is what is of interest at that time. What is unobserved may attract interest later. That buildings only show themselves partially, that the appearance of an architectural surface assumes the existence of an unseen subsurface, also means that the work's visibility can shelter an unseen potential, a set of conditions or powers that recoil from a direct approach, skipping under or slipping behind all that is grasped frontally, in order to quietly sustain what actually does appear. Again, the question posed by the recent works of Weiss and Manfredi is how this field of forces can be acknowledged without distorting it, by describing yet another set of objects or objective conditions.

Weiss and Manfredi have described their Museum of the Earth, sited in the Finger Lakes region of New York State, as an environmentally performative earthwork. A range of scales, materials, and purposes are implied in this definition, a dialogue with ambient forces. Where, for example, would one say the museum's site reaches its outer boundary? While these beautifully articulated buildings do, indeed, house the evidences of paleontological research, the project's location is not limited to (or defined by) the plot these buildings occupy, for the stratified display panels that line the ramps and interiors would

be senseless if severed from the unseen geology they represent: the laminae that extend far beyond the perimeter defined by the foundation walls. Nor does the museum's outdoor precinct circumscribe the project's outer limits, not the building's three interconnected courts (the spaces before, between, and behind the two wings), nor the parking areas aligned with the berms that direct rainwater runoff, nor even the detention pond that leads to the filtration and cleansing channel; for these elements perform their operations in the midst of a much wider field of forces, an environmental horizon from which the museum could not be severed without depriving it of the means by which many of its beautiful qualities are codetermined. We tend to assume that building sites, like things, have definite limits. The problem with this assumption is that it makes the actuality of a project like this one impossible to understand. The reshaping of the land that served as the basis for this museum did not result in the definition, but what might be called the in-definition of the building and the site. This term was used by the painter Georges Braque to describe the process of revealing an object's implicit ties to otherwise unseen elements of its vicinity.

The Museum of the Earth, like other projects by these architects, consists of incomplete volumes. Rarely in their work does the geometry of one side of the building turn a corner to form another, likewise for the elements that constitute the walls. Apertures, for example, appear, are positioned, and obtain specific size by virtue of the particular views they capture, the intensity of light they admit, and the force of wind they resist. Obviously, these conditions vary

from side to side. Instead of aligning with or repeating forms established elsewhere in the building, windows and walls develop specific relationships with the aspects of the environment they face. An exemplary case in the Museum of the Earth is the three-sided frame at the outer edge of the glacier garden. Although it calls to mind the famous viewing frame on the roof of Le Corbusier's Villa Savoye, this one's missing side allows for views that are not only frontal but lateral and descending, as if the slope that begins in the nearby clearing and ends in the distant valley has reversed its course and broken in on the very frame from which it is viewed. For Weiss and Manfredi the unity of the architectural object is less important than its interconnections with all that encompasses it. And once the "environment" is allowed to have a hand in the constitution of the building's iconography, the work's outer aspects will vary as much as its setting does. Put differently, and redefining a term Colin Rowe borrowed from André Breton, the "crisis of the object" allows for the discovery of an expanded field, topography, as the building's formative milieu. Yet, the key point is that this field is not only composed of additional, bigger, or more natural surfaces—as if the land or cityscape were just an "extra-large" building—but of powers or influences that do not appear as surfaces because their role is to force the building's several parts into visibility. Subsurfaces of this sort include environmental factors, such as wind from the northwest, daylight from the opposite direction, and driving rain from the upper hillside as well as pressures from practical events, as I will explain below. Decisive as they are in the building's definition, forces such as these only

leave their mark when architectural surfaces stand against them. With nothing to resist them, they would remain unapparent; in other words, latent. This means the building's job is to make what is latent patent—at least to some degree.

Like the Museum of the Earth, the Smith College Campus Center is composed of elements that are no less dedicated to the relationships they establish with the surrounding milieu than those they maintain with one another around the building's perimeter. The architects have stated that this project mediates the town and campus. While true, this arithmetic observation understates the project's algebraic operations, naming only two of the several conditions that enter into dialogue with the building at its margins. The building's spatial formula also takes into account a new slope to the land, from the height of the campus green to the low point on the center's side. Also factored in are contrasting "speeds" on the building's different sides: on one, a fast pace is set by a wide roadway; on another, two walkways slow the ambient tempo; and on a third, the broad lawn encourages rest. These conditions of program, terrain, and movement seem to have served as pretexts for the project's development, even though they were not particularly apparent until the building was built. On the lawn side, the campus's outer compass and inner configuration are apparent from the center's wide balcony and entry deck. The Elm Street side, by contrast, shelters some of the building's rather more private spaces behind facades with compacted depth and greater opacity, which mediate both the heavily traveled street and the relatively

small-scale domestic architecture nearby. The building's third side, diverging from Elm Street toward the center of campus, opens toward an ascending garden, shaded and secluded by a stretch of bay windows that give individuals within separate views onto the surroundings. Like the physical terrain, the topography of activities is differentiated. Just as the landscape has various qualities, so do the practical situations that are housed by the building's enclosures. As with the forces of the so-called "natural" environment, those of the inhabited or practical landscape condition the building's several surfaces, even though they do not show themselves as figures or images in their own right. The building's openings and closings, transparencies and opacities, thinnesses and thicknesses show what is given in the location by alternately accepting and resisting its advances and pressures. Precisely because they play their roles without putting themselves on show, subsurface conditions are revealed by architecture engaged with the movements and events of its milieu.

Given the site of the Barnard Nexus, it is surprising that Weiss and Manfredi have stated that "landscape" served as the project's "catalyst." Not only is the project surrounded by the dense urban fabric of New York's Upper West Side but also the building as a whole is basically a six-story prism, roughly one to five in the plan's width-to-length ratio. What's more, its bulk is aligned with the frontage and height of neighboring buildings and is similarly frontal and flat, at least on the Broadway side. The repetition of panels on the facades reinforces the initial assumption that the design was prompted by urban, not landscape conditions. Yet, if one's first

impression is of well-mannered congruity with pre-existing conditions, a second look suggests that other promptings were also influential. Look again at the cladding. The principle of repetition governs the height of the panels, no matter whether they are opaque or transparent, as each is unbroken from floor to ceiling on all of the building's levels. Yet, the widths of the panels vary—there are seven different panel dimensions, among which are multiple combinations of glass types—and their vertical stacking is irregular. Further, the ratio of solid to transparent surfaces changes according to the stepping movement of the section's public spaces, creating a diagonal across the face of the shifting grid, seen most clearly in a nighttime view. There is nothing about the urban context that prompts either the shifting of the panels or the upward climb of the public terraces. Both, one discovers, have their origin in the lawn (or landscape) that forms the heart of the campus. It, too, is a public terrace, forceful because commonly shared. And once the green is seen to have a role in shaping the building's section and articulation, its influence becomes increasingly apparent elsewhere in the building: just as one run of terraces ascends from the Lehman Lawn through the building, another steps down to the Millbank Courtyard. This outdoor walk is complemented by raised routes that emerge from within the building, pass along its side, and then return to the main volume by way of window walls that open onto distant prospects. The advance and retreat of these passages leave disturbances to the panel geometry in their wake, destabilizing the volume that initially seemed as rigid as the urban pattern. What's more, while I've described these

routes in and outside the building as independent elements, their crossings in plan and section cross out their singularity. All together, they interweave the spaces of the building into those of the campus and points in the distance. The big box does not disappear in this mix; it is endowed with unusually rich content, remote in its place of origin but discovered to be relevant nonetheless.

The difficulty of working with a nonfigurative subsurface is especially difficult when every aspect or dimension of the project is expected to present itself as a work of art. Such is the case with the recently completed Olympic Sculpture Park in Seattle. From top to bottom, all of the parts of the site are on show now that the work is done: the exhibition pavilion on Western Avenue and Broad Street, inside and out; the three archetypal landscapes (the evergreen cluster in the valley, the fragment of a deciduous forest in the grove, and the shoreline garden at the edge of Elliott Bay); as well as the entire landscape surface that joins them together, bridging the existing road and rail ways, supporting the sculptural works in all their varied situations, and easing pedestrian passage from one spot to the next across a remarkably volumetric (or variously enclosing) terrain. The net result is a surplus of imagery, abundant in quantity and rich in quality. Where, then, is the subsurface in the midst of all that is on show?

The question is made doubly difficult because not only is every part of the project put on view, but the places in the project one would tend to look for subsurface content—in the depth of the site—are soon discovered to be highly artificial, treated no less carefully than all that one sees on the surface. Consider first the underlying soil. The architects, geotechnical consultants, and civil engineers have gone to great lengths to cap and clean the toxic materials previously dumped on the site through decades of industrial use. Surfaces below are as carefully designed as those above. Likewise for the transportation infrastructure, it was organized as precisely as the green platforms that cover it. The same is true for the two miles of telecommunications network. Conditions above and below the green expanse seem equally designed. What, then— if anything—has escaped objectification? Is there a subsurface to this site, something unapparent but forceful, sufficiently forceful to qualify what has been designed in ways that might not be expected but might still be significant?

Despite all that they have designed, their exacting specifications, discerning foresight, and highly imaginative solutions to problems most architects would have judged to be unsolvable, Weiss and Manfredi have established conditions in which agencies outside their control will help define the site's visual qualities. A key to how they've done this comes from a non-architectural example, one of the park's site specific sculptural works, the Neukom Vivarium, by Mark Dion. In brief, this project involves the greenhousing of a sixty-foot western hemlock, relocated to the park from forests in the State of Washington. When the tree is seen narrowly—as an independent object—its future looks rather bleak, a "history of decay," as the writer E. M. Cioran once said. But seen differently, in its enclosure, under the heat and light

of the sun, home to countless micro-organisms, caught up in the "in-division" I described earlier, the tree can also be understood as the site of natural renewal, of the growth of a whole range of bacteria, lichen, plants, and insects, from which, the artist hopes, visitors, especially children, will learn about their region. In truth, no one can exactly predict what will emerge from the tree as it deteriorates and its offspring grows over time, but much can be expected. I believe the same is true for the park as a whole, one can imagine its future appearance, but such an image rests upon an intuition of likelihoods. Let me give an architectural example. The sloped panels that form the site's retaining walls anticipate the behavior of the topography in two ways. First, the fact that they are panels (not a monolithic wall) and that they are overlapped (not butt-jointed) shows that they expect and will allow for seismic movements and inevitable settlement (the region's geological instability is nearly as great as southern California's). A single surface or rigid wall would not remain so for long in a place such as this. Second, the panel design also takes account of the likely deposit of airborne sediments. Where they overlap, the panels create shadows that measure and animate the long surfaces. The darkness of these shadows or the contrasts they create will be enhanced over time by the deposit of airborne sediments, attracted to the joints by rougher finishes of the concrete on the shadow side. This anticipation of geology and weather is hardly passive, for the panels are also a means of participation in environmental change, like other elements in the project. Seen more broadly, design of this sort involves thinking less about the site's several figures, distinctive

as they are, than the effects they will suffer as a result of the play of ambient conditions. In short, architectural form is seen as subject to environmental definition and temporal unfolding, which are, of course, the frameworks of subsurface operations.

Weiss and Manfredi developed a number of drawings, models, and animations to visualize not only the spaces but also the schedules by which the project could meet its several programmatic requirements. The slowest configuration appears to be the one that gave the project its name: the ensemble of art works. Obviously, the collection will grow over time, but one can suppose that the site-specific works placed within the park will preserve their standing for decades. Similarly slow is the pace of change in the buildings and infrastructural networks, especially when contrasted with the movement organized by the several paths that cross the site. Faster still are the transportation routes that cut or edge the terrain (a trucking route, rail line, waterfront trolley circuit, bicycle path, and ferry line). The schema for environmental remediation introduces still another chronology into the landscape, a very long one, ranging from the unrecorded pre-history of the land's misuse, to the time of "capping," and then into the indefinite period of "monitoring." In addition to the site times that are local to the project, others serve as wider frames of reference: the schedules of business and leisure in the town that are structured by the work week and the hours of the day, the seasons of the year that regulate the growth and deterioration of the plantings, and the slow and steady rhythm of the waves against the shore. Despite the fact that I have listed these places, events, and schedules separately, their "internal"

workings require reciprocity, like the pedestrian movements that crisscross the site. I've said that both time and the environment are frameworks in which subsurface operations play themselves out. But this use of the word environment requires some qualification, for we tend to divorce the working of the natural from the human or cultural world. While commonplace, this is a disastrous dichotomy that we must endeavor to overcome, in both theory and practice. By virtue of its multiple and reciprocal temporalities, this project, like the others I've described, allows us to begin to see beyond the idea that the cultural world, or the city, is something "for us" and the natural world is something "in itself." Presented, instead, in Weiss and Manfredi's work is an ensemble of situations that give shape, schedule, and orientation to the patterns of everyday life, constituting a world that is so successful that it is taken to be natural. I'd like to call this landscape a cultural ecology, in which human affairs are synchronized with natural processes. Because the situations of everyday life are enmeshed in both the histories of a culture and the processes of the natural world, wonderful projects such as these are not only the result of architectural intuition alone but also invisible operations, which they alternately accommodate and resist. If allowed to condition the project from beneath what appears, unapparent operations will endow the work's surfaces with visual quality that far surpasses what can be designed, a truly remarkable but largely unforeseen beauty.

RECO
INFRASTRU
E
CONNEC

VERING
UCTURE:
XTENDING
IONS

CONVERSATION
DETLEF MERTINS
MARION WEISS
MICHAEL MANFREDI

Detlef Mertins: Over the past ten years you have developed a body of work and a way of working that ranges dramatically in scale from individual buildings to systems of urban infrastructure and that moves fluidly between the disciplines of architecture, landscape, and urban design. I'm fascinated by how you've teased out commonalities across these scales and among these disciplines, and at the same time, used each to rethink the other—landscape to rethink what a building is, infrastructure to rethink what a landscape is, architecture to rethink landscape, and so on.

I'd like to structure our discussion according to the themes you've articulated in grouping the projects in this book. These themes—recovering infrastructure, inhabiting landscape, and leveraging movement/vision—apply to all your work, regardless of scale, but also suggest different scales. Inhabiting suggests a smaller scale than recovering, for instance, although it could be the scale of paths, lighting, and planting in a vast landscape just as readily as the more intimate scale of building interiors. It's interesting that these themes combine nouns and verbs—nouns that have the character of master terms and verbs, like recovering, inhabiting, and leveraging, that suggest how you work as designers and how the projects perform for their users and clients.

Let's start, then, by talking about the projects that have involved urban infrastructure and former industrial lands: the Olympic Sculpture Park in Seattle, Washington for the Seattle Art Museum; the Olympic 2012 project in Queens, New York; and the Brooklyn Bridge Master Plan for the Lower Manhattan Development Corporation. What's brought you to sites of infrastructure and how do you go about recovering them?

Marion Weiss: The urban landscape is largely built over now, so there aren't many "pure" sites anymore. People are looking at places that were never considered sites for building or parks. It's no longer easy to say, "Tear down the old buildings and we'll put something fresh in." The tabula rasa approach is no longer viable. The Groundswell exhibition at the Museum of Modern Art focused on postindustrial landscapes. They're long, they're lateral, often like Seattle they're contaminated and divided by highways and trains, which means they offer less than conventional conditions as building sites. They often need to be thought of as infrastructure and landscape first and are enormous in scale and in the scale of ambition needed to make them viable parts of their cities. The space around the Brooklyn Bridge in lower Manhattan and the Seattle project are perfect examples. Every city now wants to reclaim its waterfront. But all these waterfronts are strangled by the infrastructure of trains, industry, warehouses, and highways, because cities were built from the inside out, while trade grew from the outside in. Cities now are interested in inverting that relationship. The invention of something like Battery Park City—which was all new land, all new water, instant urbanism—also wrestled with these conditions.

We speak of recovering infrastructural sites like these in the sense of rediscovering them and discovering in them potentials to become part of an urban landscape. We are interested in adding new infrastructures to them, new

landscapes, new uses, and new public life. We want to create linkages where separations now exist and slip in new uses that will integrate the site into a city's network of public spaces.

Michael Manfredi: We also look at the recovery of these sites as analogous to recovering from an illness. Our work has therapeutic value for the social and cultural health of the city.

DM: In what ways does the idea of landscape and the discipline of landscape architecture help you in this?

MW: The scale of some of the programs we've been given supports a more topological approach than the finite boundaries of many architectural projects. This is increasingly common. Landscape is a much better operative model for working in those settings than the model of a detached iconic building, which modernism used to privilege: an object removed from the land, up on pilotis. Landscapes are intriguing as models because they possess infinite sets of connections and continuities. Being of the land, the connections can even go beyond the boundaries of a project. The subsurfaces of landscapes are also very interesting. I don't just mean the dirt, but the entire geological and cultural subsurface and the latencies that can be given greater expression. We find that landscape is powerful and systemic, that it has many things going on simultaneously.

DM: The Olympic Sculpture Park is the extreme example, because it's almost all landscape and urban continuity, with very little building.

MW: And yet it's a highly assertive project, a completely invented landform, some 280,000 square feet in area, which happens to have a small 18,000-square-foot building integrated in it. We've reconstructed the entire site in order to connect parts of the city that have never been linked before.

DM: That's another way in which infrastructure, landscape, and architecture come together. With its various public spaces and zig-zag public route, constructed with retaining walls, terracing, and bridges, the park itself is a new infrastructure, overlaid on the highway and railway.

MM: We look for solutions where a relatively lean investment produces a maximum return. Like acupuncture, we look for highly specific points or moments that can galvanize a condition. We're drawn to strategies that have a certain economy and clarity. Then we try very hard to twist, push, and deform them to do more. Paradoxically, a complex project can often be designed with the lightest touch. It isn't necessarily true that the more pressures you apply to a design strategy the more complex it must be.

What's fascinating about design is it deals with economic and political constraints. Certainly we work on the formal language of our architecture, which is critical to architectural discourse. But there are also economic pressures, social pressures, certain organizational pressures when one works on a project for an extended period of time. The interaction within our office, internally, and the interaction with clients or constituencies (external) has a huge impact. One of the key things we

emphasized in Seattle was that we had to design the process as much as the project. The less defined the projects are in the first instance, the more important it is to shape the process or know how to intervene in any process that is already underway. As far as evaluating whether a work is good or whether a particular strategy has value, a work is good if it can withstand all of these pressures.

MW: On an urban level, we often think back to the desire for multiple layers that was embedded in Le Corbusier's work and in all those megastructural visions that never got built. Everybody wanted to multiply the ground plane, to realize a city with multiple layers. Think of Hugh Ferris's visionary drawings of Manhattan from the 1920s, with all of these elevated bridges. The multiplication of the urban level has always been a goal. That multiplication did actually take place but with greater differentiation than architects had envisioned (a highway here, a local road there, a public terrain here).

In designing urban landscapes, our approach is similar to designing buildings but also different. One thing that's very different is that your constituency, and the group that needs to be convinced to invest in it, is enormous. If it's in New Orleans, for instance, the stakeholders include all the community groups as well as engineers, insurance people, mayors, governors, federal agencies, etc. When the constituent groups become so broad and money is at stake, design can create a common ground for everyone, which nothing else can do, and that's exciting. A design can establish consensus and then people can critique parts. That's when listening becomes interesting because

when everyone's ideas or aims get embedded, people feel ownership and are more invested in seeing something realized. Design has the capacity to resolve competing interests and agendas that often can't be resolved in words. We find that an enormous diversity of agendas can somehow operate within a design but it is essential to not only shape the direction, but also shape a set of convictions that allow it to be realized.

DM: Listening in that way not only facilitates the realization of the project, but it also means that once the project is realized it's capable of performing in many different ways because you've absorbed so much in the design. It's going to have multiple values and effects that address different audiences.

MM: I think that's actually another way of gauging success: how many different audiences or how many different strata (social, economic) can it reach. The other way to see the success of a project is if it reaches a constituency that wasn't even at the table. Often that's the case in large, highly contested projects. That constituency may be out there and needs to have a voice. We've always been drawn to projects that have a social dimension; we hope that what we do is of value to constituencies that can't afford to participate in the discussions.

DM: As you design, aren't you also asking yourself questions about the project's likely performance in terms that are quite specific? Such as, "How can we open up a view or create a line of movement that doesn't exist, or allow something to be experienced in a new way, or produce a specific economic or political effect?"

MW: What we're looking for is robustness and resilience. In engineering for instance, elegance is reached when something's fully optimized and you've been able to limit the physical weight (especially in aerospace), the number of connections, the materials, and the number of opportunities for things to fall apart through entropy. On the space shuttle the tile skin, a collection of many separate units, increased the potential for failure. Arguably, you could say that we seek a few strategic devices that to do many things. You can see this in our early models for the Seattle project. We try to identify a diagram or a resilient form that's so simple that it can withstand the inevitable changes in program and the obligations of value engineering, which pulls costs out of the project while still maintaining the value in it. A design strategy must be durable and robust to survive.

DM: You are known as great collaborators. When you worked on projects like New York's bid for the 2012 Olympics, you found yourself at the center of a huge public process with many players. How did your skills as an architect serve in bringing people and agendas together on projects of that scale? How do they enable you to be leaders in such processes?

MM: The role of synthetic thinking is crucial. The irony about the Olympics is that it presented a very clearly defined set of needs: how to house the Olympic Games. But by placing those needs on a site that defied clarity, it forced everyone to rethink the program and the conventional ideas of sports and entertainment. That forced us to think of the questions not asked...the kind of questions that usually fall in the cracks between disciplines.

You have to be synthetic to avoid those disciplinary boundaries. We often work with a large group of specialists—planners, structural engineers, traffic engineers, graphic designers, wetland ecologists, and more—who see a particular condition in terms of their own disciplinary worlds. Our education as architects, and certainly the way we work, has forced us to think laterally and to see what relationships exist. We don't begin with a preconceived idea and don't use a linear, top-down approach. It's essential to bring lateral relationships and peripheral vision into the process.

MW: In these urban areas, conventional master planning—analysis of traffic flow, program uses, wet/dry areas, parking, public/private zones—often produces something that's not terribly interesting and often doesn't get realized because it hasn't had the intensity of research that architectural design often does. What we do with these large urban landscapes is exactly what we do with a building. We begin with an intense amount of research into all the different pre-existing conditions, operations, and presences. In the case of the Olympics, these presences included highway interchanges and overpasses and groundwater that used to be above grade until it was forced below grade with landfill. Our research lets us recognize what's worth giving presence to and what can be effectively leveraged. We are pretty good listeners, not just in the sense that we've learned to listen but that we listen hard because there's usually some other fabulous thing that we hadn't been aware of and can use to make the design richer and stronger. Once you find that, all of a sudden it's exciting to embed it, use it, and energize the design with it. So listening is actually energizing, particularly when you've reached a certain point where the design needs some new insight. It could come from a community meeting or from a contractor saying, "The price of steel has gone up too much." Making architecture teaches you to take advantage of the many voices and issues that impinge on a project, and that skill is transferable to the larger scale.

MM: This may be true for anything creative, but it's particularly true in the context of large projects where there are multiple agendas, like the Olympics, Seattle, or our work downtown for the Lower Manhattan Development Corporation (LMDC). The question that isn't asked, for either overt or covert reasons, becomes, for us, the stimulant for a really interesting design approach. For the Olympics, everybody was talking about the requirements of sports, but nobody asked the ecological question: "When placed here, what's the impact going to be on this highly contested site?" And that issue became in many ways the driving force behind our design strategy, rather than the particulars of how many boats you can position on the lake. In the LMDC project, the overriding concern was security but nobody said, "This is an extremely strategic place (the Brooklyn Bridge), since it lies at the intersection of four or five very different micro-cities. How can they start to rub up against each other and reconnect?" Those unasked questions became the catalyst for our design strategy.

I think designers today are responding to several really significant shifts or pressures. There may be more, but the

two that stand out are the redefinition or dissolution of what's public and private; that becomes very interesting for thinking through issues of program, spatial effects, and the tension between landscape and architecture. The other is ecology. We have an obligation to think those through in novel ways as designers, not to be glib or presume that if you simply introduce recycled materials a building will be more ecological.

What's really interesting about ecological concerns is that they demand thinking in terms of process and the interrelationship of different processes. That sense of process has entered into a lot of what we and our contemporaries are trying to reconcile spatially as designers—how to think about ecological concerns inventively and freshly.

DM: Reclaiming infrastructural sites involves natural, technological, and social systems—remediating contamination and reactivating natural systems that have been eroded, while integrating new kinds of public uses where they have been excluded. What you're describing is in effect a way of operating within social and natural ecologies at the same time. It's interesting that the words ecology and economy share a common root. How does a dynamic and temporal understanding of these sites and their operative ecological and social systems inform your approach to design or the research you do? As you start working on new sites, what are the ways in which you study and analyze them, and what are the things you draw on to begin to structure a response?

MM: The process is iterative, in the sense that you can never (as might have been implied) simply read a site because as soon as you do you intervene and change the context. That's pretty well understood in scientific inquiry. By intervening you destabilize the context and in so doing you make something new, something novel. So the sense of starting with a significant analysis is important but that doesn't mean that a clear and logical design will grow out of that. The process is quite a bit messier. We immerse ourselves in the site, the context, in order to define it as a particular condition, a moment in time, and a set of opportunities. In looking for a project for the Olympics in Queens we picked apart a number of specific strands, cultural as well as geological, hydrological as well as infrastructural.

DM: I've been struck that you often use a timeline to see the evolution and transformation of those sites and other aspects of the contexts for your projects.

MM: Yes, actually a timeline is a valuable tool to remind ourselves that our intervention is, in turn, part of another set of histories or conditions, a new set of realities that might become fertile ground for further change.

Intuitively we are drawn to the sense that we are a part of a large set of continuous events that are always interacting with each other, so even the design process is highly iterative. We're fairly promiscuous about throwing out ideas, or types, or strategies, and then seeing how they initiate the frictions or overlaps that emerge as you test them against the various sites (cultural, ecological, historic).

As a methodology it's the way we work. We recognize that there isn't a teleological process from analysis to finished project (a modernist fiction). The idea that you start with analysis and then develop the project as a reflection of the analysis is a myth. Design can lead to unexpected and welcome surprises.

MW: The timelines we make seem to be very clear and linear, which is important for describing the research to others, but the processes they record are anything but direct. The research for Seattle not only looked at its geologic history and its man-made history but also at the history of sculpture, the history of earthworks, and the idea of public landscapes. While all of this research was being done (both off-site as well as on-site) we started a parallel work of making physical models, working literally with the surface of Strathmore board: folding, cutting, bending, manipulating, etc. These architectural studies happen at the same time, simply and tentatively. (It's not as if there is an incubation period of research—doing all the historical reading, understanding the context—and then a leap into making.) The many simple models that we make constitute another line of research. Arguably both create an environment that lets us operate intuitively on many threads simultaneously as opposed to singularly. Our preoccupation with connectivity is physical at the scale of the sites, but we also see ourselves connecting different contexts through our design process.

OLYMPIC SCULPTURE PARK
SEATTLE, WASHINGTON

Emblematic of many post industrial cities, Seattle is disconnected from its waterfront by transportation infrastructure. The site of the Seattle Art Museum's Olympic Sculpture Park, an 8.5-acre former industrial site sliced into three separate parcels by train tracks and a four lane arterial road, overlooks Elliott Bay in Puget Sound. The design, a continuous constructed landscape for art, transforms the city's connection to the water by rising over the existing infrastructure to reconnect the urban core to a revitalized waterfront.

The park unfolds as a continuous Z-shaped landscape that wanders from the city to the bay, alternately revealing and concealing the train and roadways below. This hybrid landform provides a new pedestrian infrastructure layered over the existing site with a system of mechanically stabilized earth and capitalizes on the forty-foot grade change from the top of the hill to the water's edge. The enhanced earthwork reestablishes the original topography of the site, as it crosses the highway and train tracks and descends to meet the water—a chameleon-like strategy that begins as a fully emerged form (a hilltop pavilion) and concludes in a fully submerged condition (a shoreline garden with aquatic terraces that form a regenerative underwater habitat for fish and plant life).

The 2,200-foot-long pedestrian route begins at the 12,000-square-foot multi-use pavilion from which visitors traverse the site on a pathway that establishes topographic variations and open up radically different prospects. The first leg crosses the highway, offering vistas of

Elliott Bay and the Olympic Mountains; the second, on axis with Mount Rainer, spans the train tracks, providing visual connections to the city, port, and mountain; and the third descends to the water, offering views of the newly created beach. This pedestrian infrastructure allows free movement, long denied, between downtown Seattle and the newly created beach at the base of the site. The tilting planes of the Z-shaped landform define a series of microsettings, each a diverse ecological environment of native plantings. As the crushed-stone path descends from the pavilion to the water, it links three landscapes indigenous to the Northwest: a dense and temperate evergreen forest lined with ferns; a deciduous forest of quaking aspens with seasonally changing characteristics; and a shoreline garden with tidal terraces for salmon habitat and saltwater vegetation. The landform and plantings collaborate to direct, collect, and cleanse stormwater as it travels down the site and is released into Elliott Bay.

Throughout the site seemingly parallel lines converge, accentuating the laws of perspective to suggest infinite distances within the confines of the park. The primary diagonals link the city and bay along the Z-shaped landform. Secondary diagonals mediate the vertical section of the site, emerging from the surrounding city and ascending to cross the highway and train lines and reach the new elevated terrain. The rhythm of overlapping concrete retaining walls provides a metering device that links architecture, earthwork, landscape, and art.

At the top of the park the pavilion, which appears to hover over its parking

structure base, accommodates art installations, performances, and educational programming beneath its cantilevered roof. The pavilion, designed as an extension of the landscape, unfolds to offer views of the waterfront. Its split section extends the diagonal movement of the Z-path up to an elevated mezzanine that overlooks the park, Elliott Bay, and the Olympic Mountains. The concrete walls and diagonal steel roof structure continues the scale and meter of the park's bridges and retaining walls into the pavilion. Its glass and stainless-steel facades reflect and intensify the urban surroundings and appear ephemeral at sunset, when the building absorbs the gold and pink colors of dusk. At night, the pavilion becomes a luminous presence within the park and the city, providing a terminus to the runway of lights that dot the pedestrian path.

An amphitheater provides a transition from the pavilion to a valley, where Richard Serra's Wake is sited. The Z-path bridges the roadway and descends to the waterfront, passing views of Mark Dion's Neukom Vivarium, Calder's emblematic Eagle, and Tony Smith's Stinger. Beneath it all, new subsurface infrastructure provides continuous power, water, and telephone and data lines that allow artists to incorporate sophisticated technologies into their work.

The Olympic Sculpture Park rethinks the conventions of the typical sculpture park, providing a dynamic and evolving setting for art. Several site-specific works commissioned by the museum were integrated into the project's design and construction; exhibitions of iconic modern sculptures from private collections are carefully positioned and temporary installations are commissioned on an ongoing basis.

As a landscape for art, the Olympic Sculpture Park extends the experience of viewing modern and contemporary works beyond the museum walls. Illuminating the power of an invented landscape to create connections between art and ecology, city and waterfront, the deliberately open-ended design invites new interpretations of art, ecology, and urban engagement.

22

Geology

Seattle

Art in the
Landscape

program + art

vegetation + art

paths + art

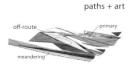

city + art

water + art

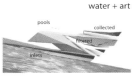

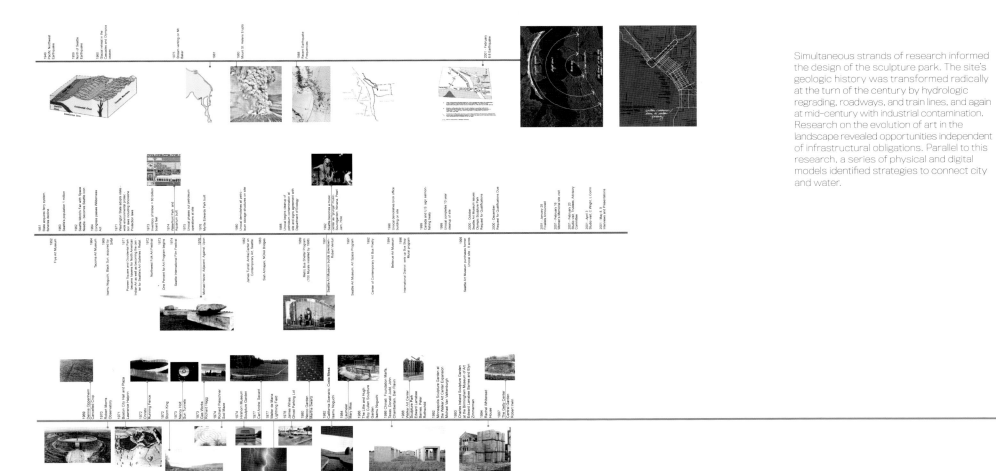

Simultaneous strands of research informed the design of the sculpture park. The site's geologic history was transformed radically at the turn of the century by hydrologic regrading, roadways, and train lines, and again at mid-century with industrial contamination. Research on the evolution of art in the landscape revealed opportunities independent of infrastructural obligations. Parallel to this research, a series of physical and digital models identified strategies to connect city and water.

23

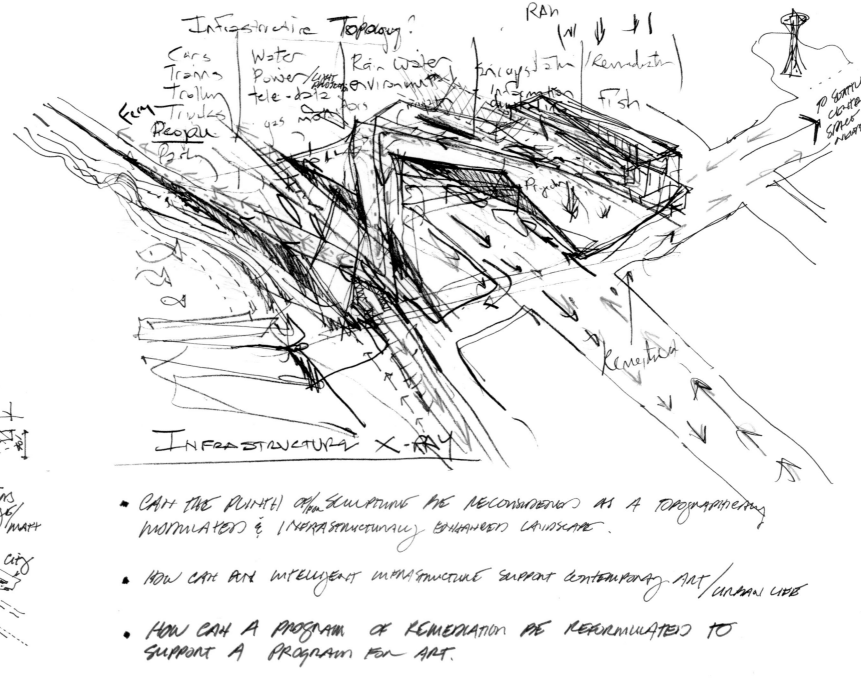

Infrastructure Topology?

Cars
Trams
Trollies
Trucks
People
Party

Water
Power/Light
tele-data
gas

Rain Water
Environment

Ecosystem/Remediation

Fish

RAIN

To Seattle Center Spaces Nearby

From

Projected

Remediation

INFRASTRUCTURE X-RAY

GAP AS SPONGE/MATT

CITY

WATER

- CAN THE PLINTH OR/FOR SCULPTURE BE RECONSIDERED AS A TOPOGRAPHICALLY MODULATED & INFRASTRUCTURALLY ENHANCED LANDSCAPE.

- HOW CAN AN INTELLIGENT INFRASTRUCTURE SUPPORT CONTEMPORARY ART/URBAN LIFE

- HOW CAN A PROGRAM OF REMEDIATION BE REFORMULATED TO SUPPORT A PROGRAM FOR ART.

Three former industrial sites, located
between downtown Seattle and
the waters of Elliott Bay, were separated
by roadways and rail lines. The design
strategy, a Z-shaped landform, connects
these sites and unfolds from the city
to the water's edge.

The constructed landforms, linked
by two bridges, form a continuous
topography that descends
forty-feet from the city to the newly
created beach.

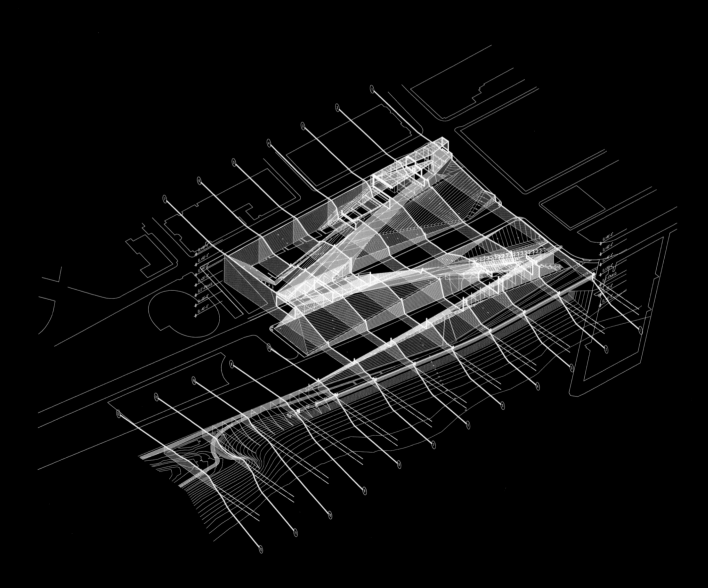

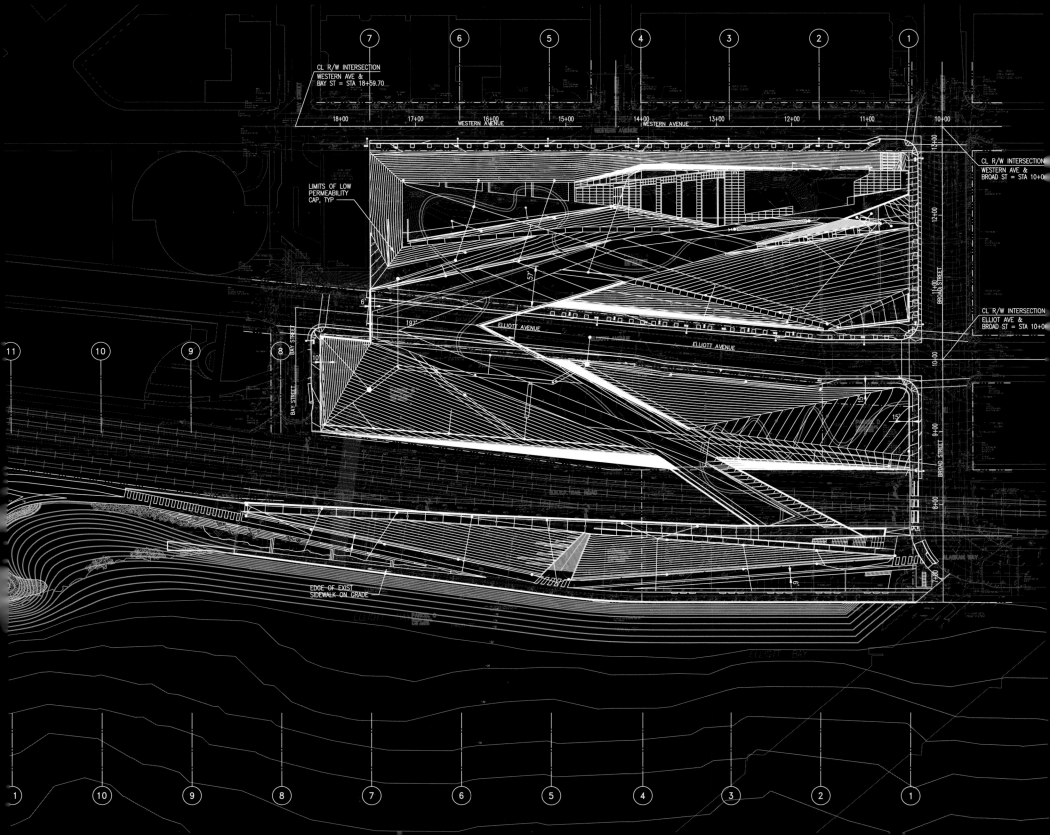

**LANDSCAPE & ART
PROGRAM PRECINCTS**

 turf : structured art precinct
 meadow : flexible art precinct
groundcover : flexible art precinct
 beach : environmental art precinct

 evergreen grove

deciduous grove

INFRASTRUCTURAL NETWORKS

 bollard lighting
power/teledata/security conduits

HARDSCAPE & PATHS

 primary path
secondary path
tertiary path

DRAINAGE & MARINE OUTFALL

 surface drainage
subsurface drainage

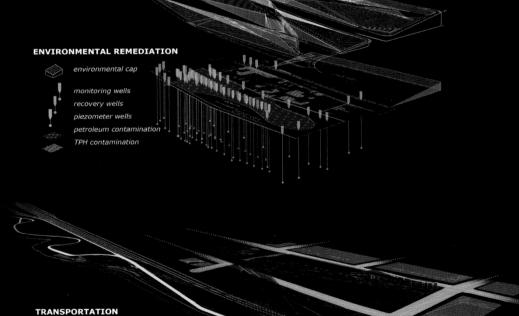

Each layer of the park meets distinctly different demands: art, landscape, and infrastructure are superimposed over remediation systems, drainage collection, and existing transportation routes. With nearly two miles of subsurface power, teledata, and water, these layers together create a resilient and flexible framework for future art installations.

ENVIRONMENTAL REMEDIATION

- environmental cap
- monitoring wells
- recovery wells
- piezometer wells
- petroleum contamination
- TPH contamination

TRANSPORTATION

- Federal Trucking route
- BNSF/Amtrak railways
- Seattle Waterfront Trolley
- bicycle path
- ferry line

Two hundred sixty thousand cubic yards of earth were sculpted to create the landforms that define the connecting topography.

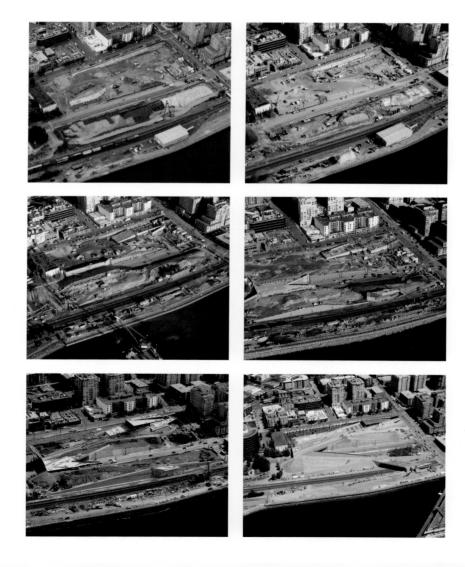

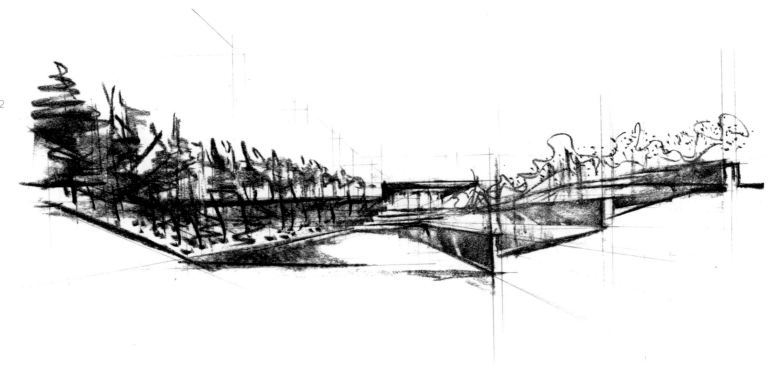

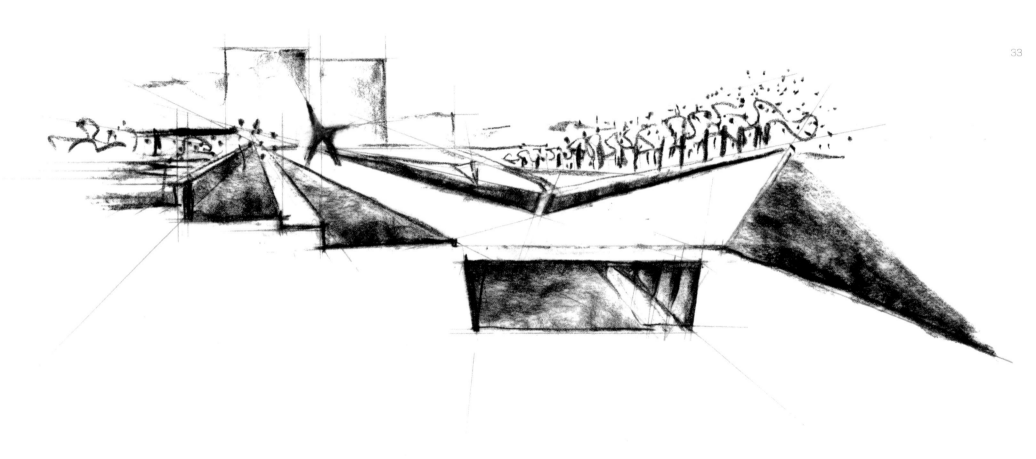

38

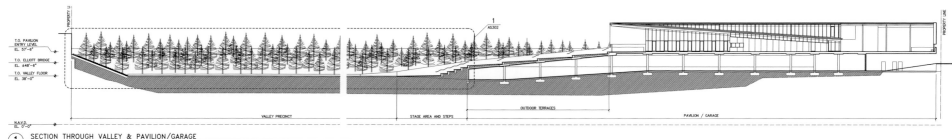

T.O. PAVILION
ENTRY LEVEL
EL. 57'-6"

T.O. ELLIOTT BRIDGE
EL. ±48'-6"

T.O. VALLEY FLOOR
EL. 38'-0"

N.A.V.D.
EL. 0'-0"

VALLEY PRECINCT   STAGE AREA AND STEPS   OUTDOOR TERRACES   PAVILION / GARAGE

1   SECTION THROUGH VALLEY & PAVILION/GARAGE
    1" = 20'

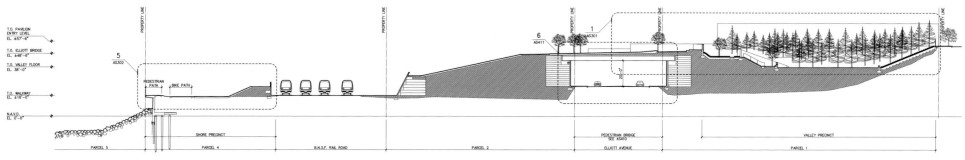

T.O. PAVILION
ENTRY LEVEL
EL. ±57'-6"

T.O. ELLIOTT BRIDGE
EL. ±48'-6"

T.O. VALLEY FLOOR
EL. 38'-0"

T.O. WALKWAY
EL. ±16'-0"

N.A.V.D.
EL. 0'-0"

PEDESTRIAN
PATH   BIKE PATH

PARCEL 5   SHORE PRECINCT   PARCEL 4   B.N.S.F. RAIL ROAD   PARCEL 2   PEDESTRIAN BRIDGE
SEE AS410   ELLIOTT AVENUE   VALLEY PRECINCT   PARCEL 1

2   CROSS SECTION THROUGH ELLIOTT AVENUE BRIDGE
    1" = 20'

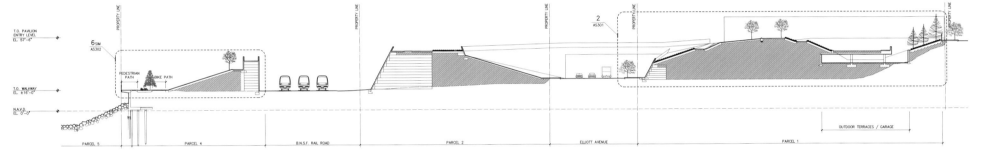

T.O. PAVILION
ENTRY LEVEL
EL. 57'-6"

6 SIM
AS302

PEDESTRIAN
PATH   BIKE PATH

T.O. WALKWAY
EL. ±16'-0"

N.A.V.D.
EL. 0'-0"

PROPERTY LINE   PROPERTY LINE   PROPERTY LINE   PROPERTY LINE   PROPERTY LINE

2
AS301

OUTDOOR TERRACES / GARAGE

PARCEL 5   PARCEL 4   B.N.S.F. RAIL ROAD   PARCEL 2   ELLIOTT AVENUE   PARCEL 1

3 | CROSS SECTION THROUGH EAGLE STREET
1" = 20'

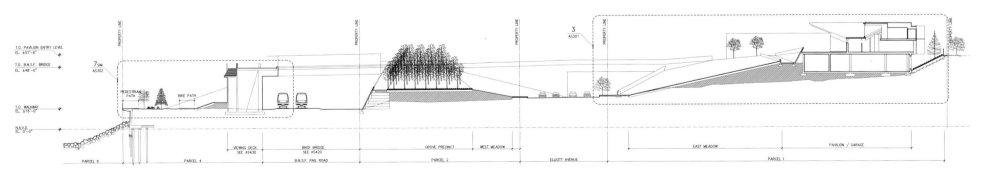

T.O. PAVILION ENTRY LEVEL
EL. ±57'-6"

T.O. B.N.S.F. BRIDGE
EL. ±48'-0"

7 SIM
AS302

PEDESTRIAN
PATH   BIKE PATH

T.O. WALKWAY
EL. ±16'-0"

N.A.V.D.
EL. 0'-0"

PROPERTY LINE   PROPERTY LINE   PROPERTY LINE   PROPERTY LINE

3
AS301

VIEWING DECK   BNSF BRIDGE   GROVE PRECINCT   WEST MEADOW   EAST MEADOW   PAVILION / GARAGE
SEE AS430   SEE AS420

PARCEL 6   PARCEL 4   B.N.S.F. RAIL ROAD   PARCEL 2   ELLIOTT AVENUE   PARCEL 1

4 | CROSS SECTION THROUGH PAVILION & ALASKAN WAY ENTRY PLAZA
1" = 20'

The shifting planes of the site design
establish distinct precincts that create
topographically varied settings for art.
Richard Serra's **Wake** is sited amongst
terraced zones for smaller sculptural
works. Alexander Calder's **Eagle** serves
as the visual icon for the park and is
perched over Elliott Avenue and seen
in silhouette against the horizon.

40

Both the plan and section of the park pavilion share the geometry of the Z-path. Compressed at the entry, the pavilion expands in width and height to open to views of the waterfront and accommodate large scale artwork. The pavilion contains a café; a multipurpose space for performance, lectures, events, and exhibition; offices; and a parking garage in the lower level.

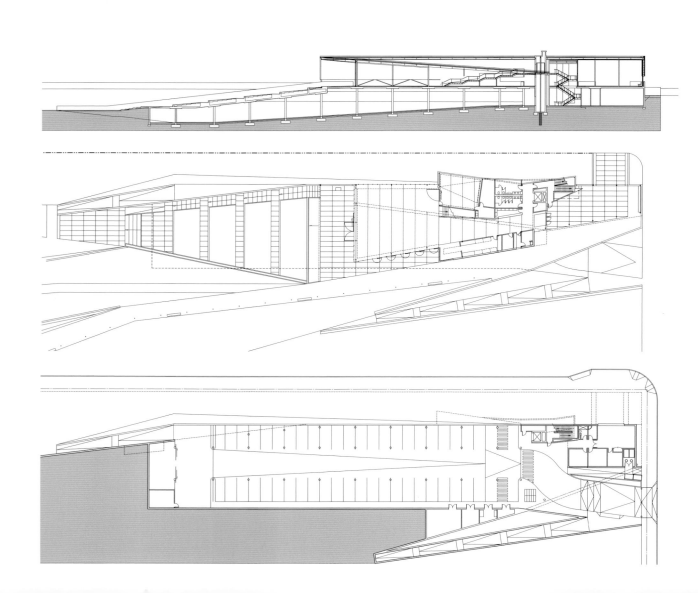

50 The Seattle Art Museum invited artists
    to propose permanent projects to be
    built into the concept and structure of the
    park, initiating a series of collaborations
    between artist and architect. Richard Serra
    worked closely with the design team to
    choose the most appropriate site for **Wake**.
    A sequence of design adjustments were
    made to clarify the geometry of the valley
    precinct relative to the final placement
    of this piece.

Mark Dion worked with the design team to select a site at the edge of the park to create his **Neukom Vivarium**. The trapezoidal structure comments on the geometry of the park and houses an eighty-foot hemlock nursing log that is the centerpiece of the installation. The green-glazed roof simulates the light filtering effect of the forest canopy and creates a functional environment for this artwork.

Regulations for bridging the Burlington Northern Santa Fe rail line through the park required a "throw fence" and canopy along the bridge edge. Artist Teresita Fernandez utilized the frame for this fence as a point of departure for her piece. Working closely with the artist, Weiss/Manfredi created a structure for **Seattle Cloud Cover**, a mural of laminated glass panels showing a transparent, multicolored image of a fictional horizon.

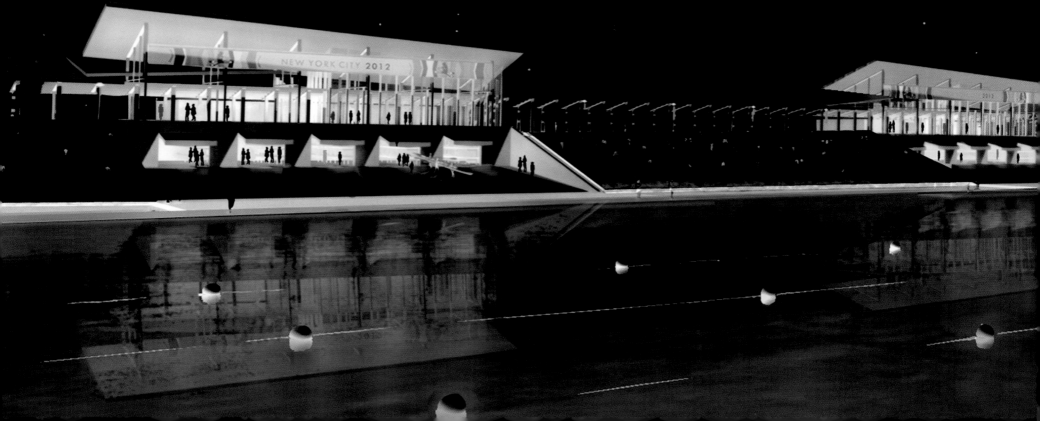

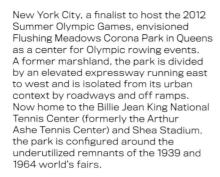

NYC2012
FLUSHING MEADOWS CORONA PARK, QUEENS, NEW YORK

New York City, a finalist to host the 2012 Summer Olympic Games, envisioned Flushing Meadows Corona Park in Queens as a center for Olympic rowing events. A former marshland, the park is divided by an elevated expressway running east to west and is isolated from its urban context by roadways and off ramps. Now home to the Billie Jean King National Tennis Center (formerly the Arthur Ashe Tennis Center) and Shea Stadium, the park is configured around the underutilized remnants of the 1939 and 1964 world's fairs.

The design for the Olympic white water and flat water rowing venues, done in collaboration with Laurie Olin, transforms the preexisting infrastructure and the lakes and reflecting pools into a new recreational and ecological landscape. Two elevated boardwalks, set beneath the Piranesian expressway ramps, sit within a new wetlands terrain that captures storm water and supports new plant and wildlife habitats. The intent of the site design is to offer a post-Olympics legacy that brings coherence to the park's component parts.

Located eight hundred feet east of the Unisphere, the icon of the 1964 world's fair, a former circular reflecting pool is reconfigured as a bermed, spiral-shaped venue for white water rowing events and elevated twenty-six feet to ensure adequate velocity and turbulence along the competition course. Recirculation pumps carry the water back to the highest launch point, where a media pavilion becomes a new overlook for the park. The interior face of the spiral provides seating for fifteen thousand people.

The berm's perimeter offers views onto nearby public soccer fields. A network of paths and berms provide post-Olympic uses, including biking, skateboarding, and in-line skating.

Two existing lakes on the south side of the park have been connected to meet the requirements of the two thousand-meter (6,562-foot) flat water rowing competition events. An elevated peninsula divides the competition course from the practice course and becomes the site for a series of new boathouses and floating docks. The peninsula's continuous grass berms provide overflow seating for spectators. The peninsula also divides the north end of the lake into a slender practice course and the full-length competition course. Future uses for the boathouses and water courses include competitive rowing as well as recreational boating.

Connecting the north and south halves of the park, a new wetlands landscape—characterized by bull rushes, regal ferns, and water horsetail—reinstates the habitat that thrived a century ago when the site was a marshland. Superimposed over this landscape are a pair of curved boardwalks that link the white water and flat water venues, their configuration inspired by the arc of overhead on and off ramps. The design for the park and its Olympic events recasts the leftover landscapes of infrastructure and world's fairs into a dramatic and ecologically sensitive public setting.

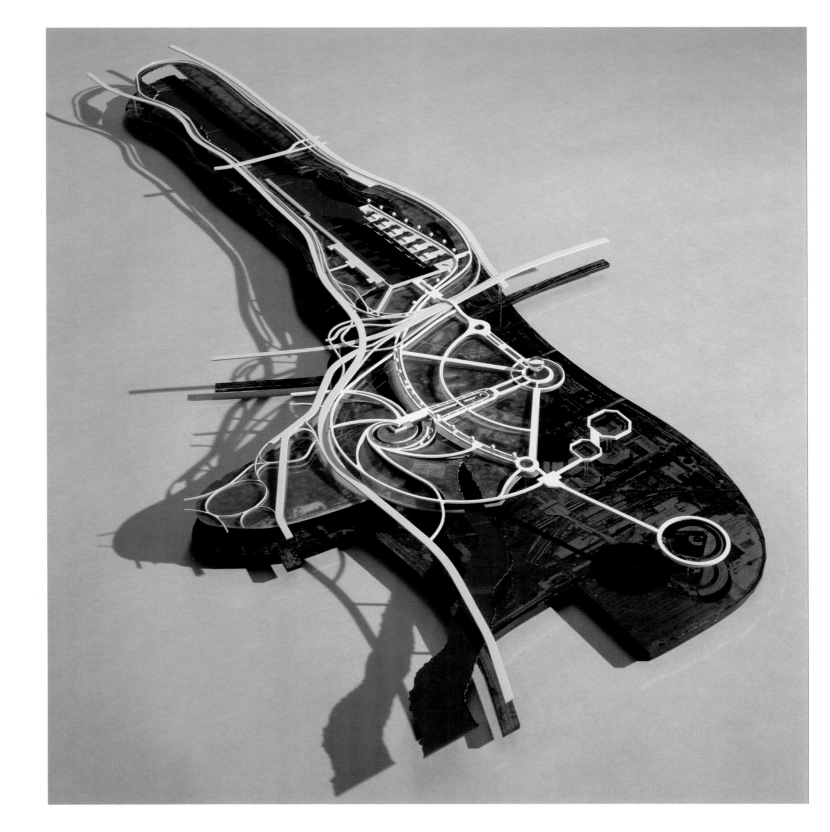

Originally a vast wetland bordering Flushing Bay, the site of Flushing Meadows Corona Park has been crisscrossed with transportation networks and reconceived for two world's fairs. The new master plan takes advantage of the Olympic athletic programs to reconnect the park, reintroduce the former wetland ecosystem, create new settings for recreation, and reveal the varied histories of the site.

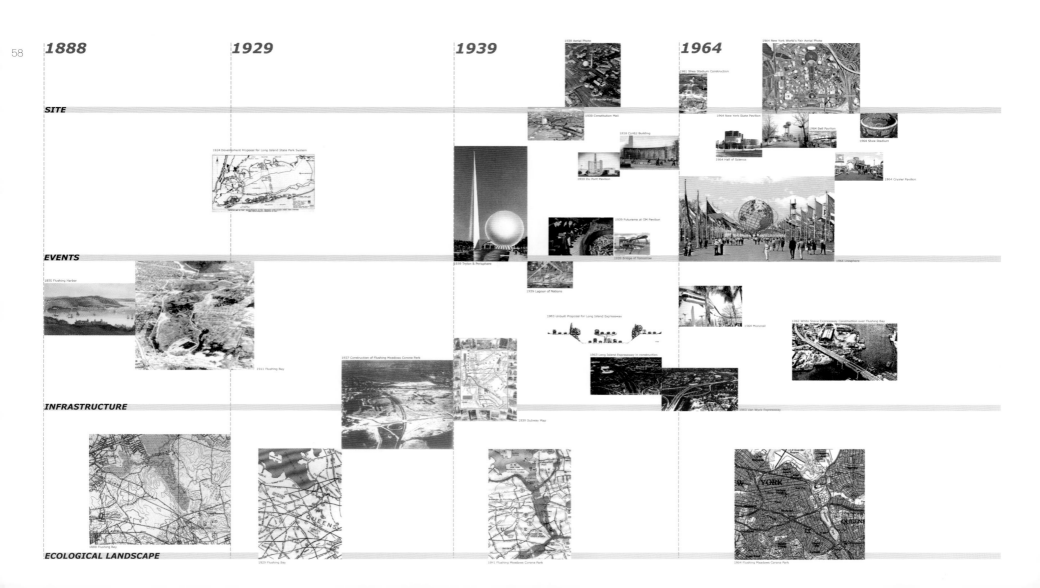

1888   **1929**   **1939**   **1964**

SITE

EVENTS

INFRASTRUCTURE

ECOLOGICAL LANDSCAPE

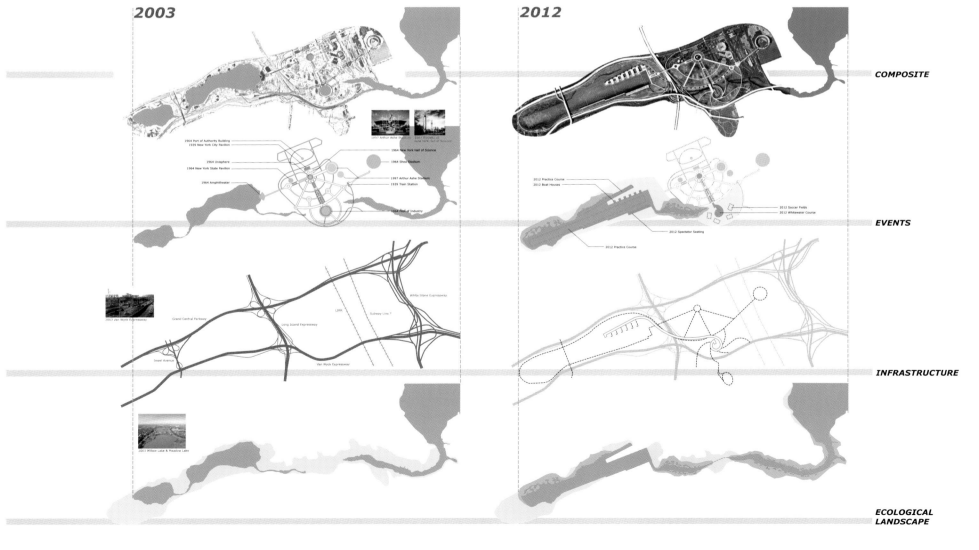

2003

2012

COMPOSITE

EVENTS

INFRASTRUCTURE

*ECOLOGICAL
LANDSCAPE*

60 Three separate bodies of water are relinked
to Flushing Bay with a new network of canals
and wetlands. Olympic rowing facilities
designed for the NYC2012 will be converted
for subsequent public recreational use.

Located along a major coastal flyway, New York City parks provide habitat for a stunning variety of avian species. Reintroduced wetlands increase roosting sites while providing habitat for aquatic and terrestrial species. Above this new ecological infrastructure, pedestrian pathways link areas of the park now separated by elevated highways.

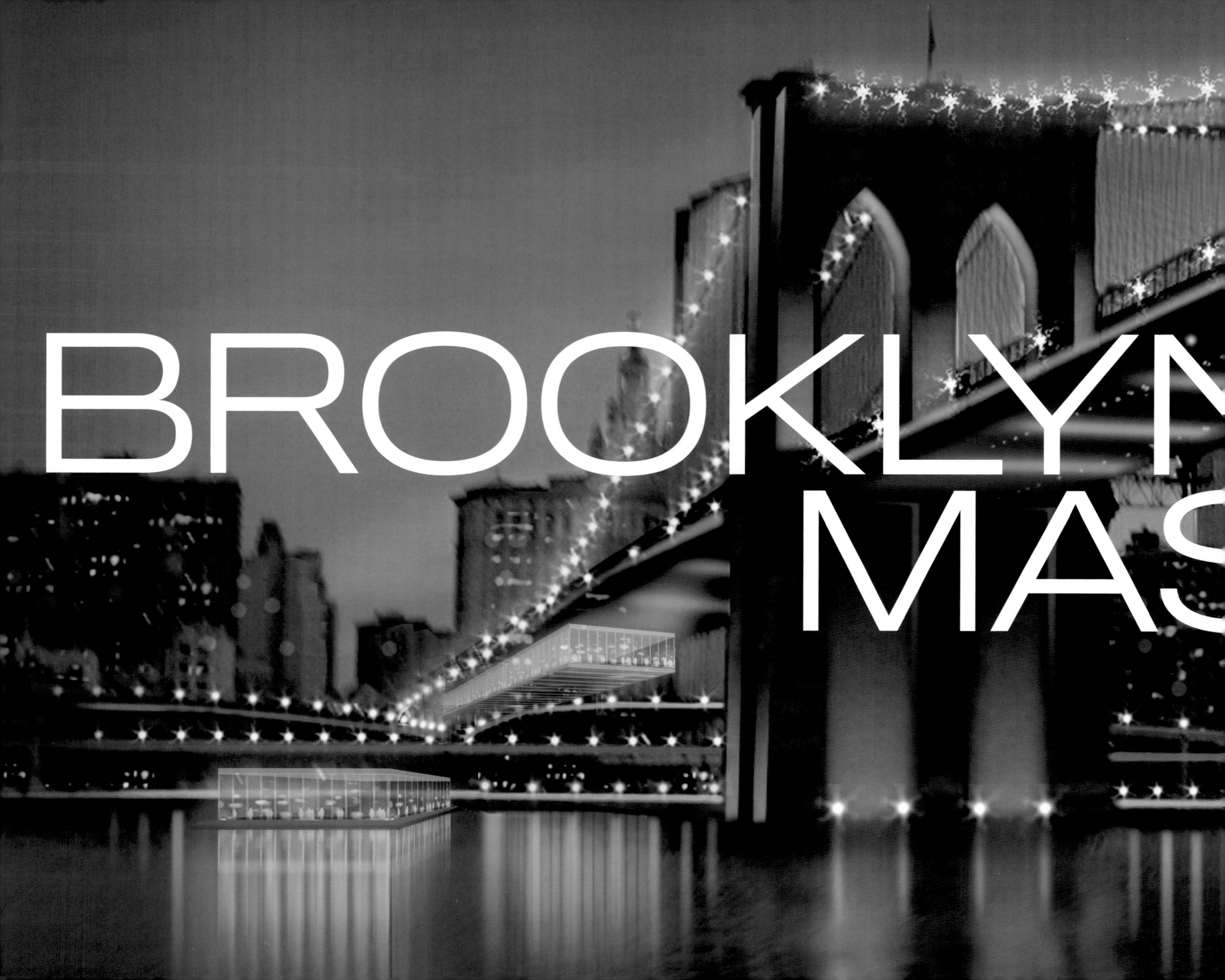
BROOKLYN
MAS

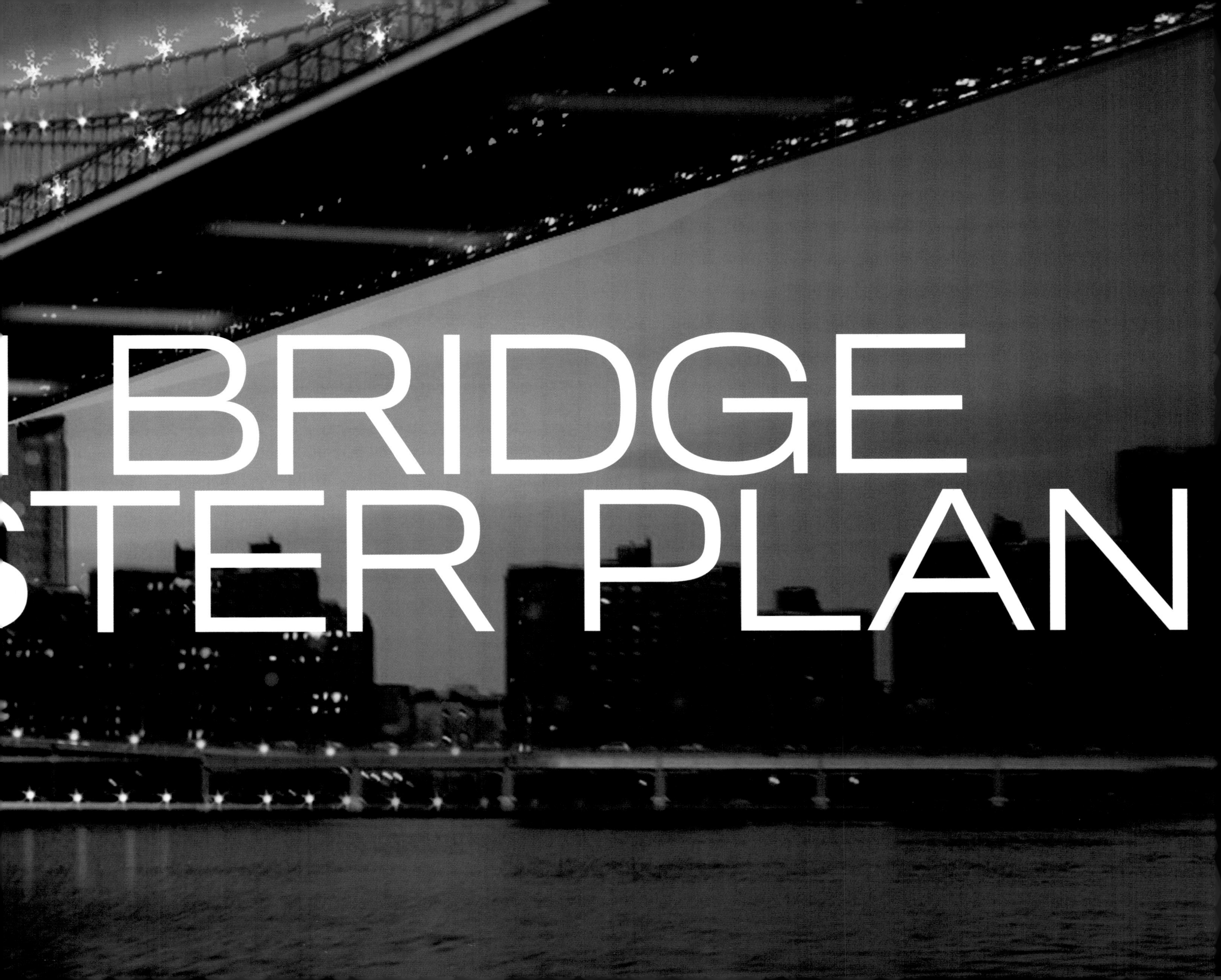
BRIDGE
STER PLAN

BROOKLYN BRIDGE MASTER PLAN
NEW YORK, NEW YORK

Urban infrastructures—bridges, highways, on and off ramps—often create barriers and uninhabitable spaces where they meet the ground plane. This phenomenon is evident in Lower Manhattan, where the anchorage and vehicular distribution network of the Brooklyn Bridge have imposed profound divisions between neighborhoods north and south of the span.

The area surrounding the bridge supports a residential and commuter population of more than fifty thousand people and is defined by Chinatown to the north, the Financial District to the south, city hall to the west and the East River to the east. The entrance to the bridge is hemmed in by a network of on and off ramps that preclude future development in the area.

The challenges of this area were exacerbated following the terrorist attacks of September 11, 2001. Street closings—meant to increase security in this important civic precinct that include the municipal building, city hall, and the police headquarters—have had the unfortunate effect of impeding vehicular and pedestrian circulation. New security issues raised by the existing police headquarters near the base of the bridge led to the creation of new barriers undermining the already frail pedestrian and roadway connections to the north and south.

The scope of this study includes improvements to vehicular and pedestrian connections between Chinatown and the Financial District, the introduction of new programs, and the innovative reuse of the orphaned sites created by the maze of bridge ramps and the FDR Drive, which separates the city from the river's

edge. The study recommends that these sites be stitched together through the introduction of three new north to south transects, which vary in character and purpose. Together, they make coherent links between the communities north and south of the bridge and help animate the area around its anchorage.

The East River Transect reprograms the abandoned space under the elevated FDR Drive with athletic uses and proposes to connect into the jogging and pedestrian paths that currently flank the river. A new pocket beach marks the intersection of the East River Transect and the bridge. The second link, known as the Pearl Street Transect, connects the South Street Seaport retail area and the Lower Manhattan Ferry Terminal to the south with Chinatown and Union Square to the north. This transect is envisioned as an active urban corridor that extends the vibrancy and street life of Chinatown through new lighting and retail spaces and reconfigured street edges. Finally, the Park Row–to–City Hall Transect is envisioned as a green corridor, a bi-level ribbon of open spaces that connects the elevated police headquarters plaza and the municipal building to Chinatown. This ascending earthwork simultaneously provides enhanced security to the police building and introduces critical new pedestrian connections.

The study also recommends that a luminous structure be built into the vaulted anchorage of the Brooklyn Bridge and extend as an elevated structure overlooking on and off ramps and the East River. This new linear construction creates spaces for retail, restaurants,

offices, and athletic facilities and animates the masonry vaults of the anchorage and the interstitial zone of the dramatic bridge trusses. The massive scale of the span's structure presents an opportunity to harbor a finer grain of spaces and activities.

The study proposes site-specific strategies to link downtown areas that have become disconnected by the presence of the bridge and post-9/11 road closings. By reinventing new spatial strategies for the ramp infrastructure, capitalizing on the scale and landmark status of the Brooklyn Bridge, and leveraging the realities of increased security, the proposed new strategy transforms the monofunctional presence of infrastructure into a new paradigm for urban intervention.

After 9/11, road closures for pedestrian and vehicular traffic made most of the area surrounding the Brooklyn Bridge in Manhattan impassable. New understandings of the site evolved from analysis of the surrounding communities; municipal, commercial and recreational zones; and vehicular and pedestrian routes.

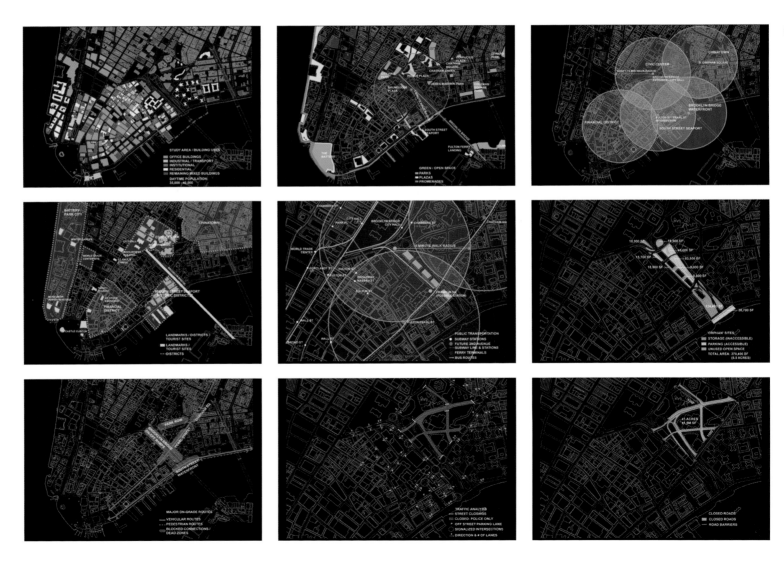

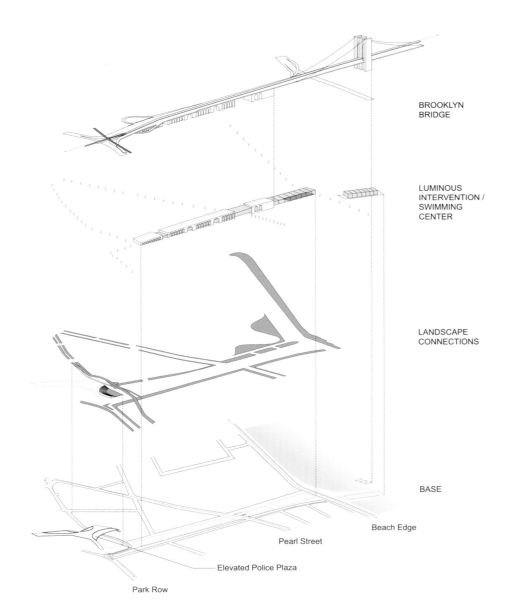

BROOKLYN
BRIDGE

LUMINOUS
INTERVENTION /
SWIMMING
CENTER

LANDSCAPE
CONNECTIONS

BASE

Beach Edge

Pearl Street

Elevated Police Plaza

Park Row

A phased plan of layered interventions
opens and illuminates the Brooklyn
Bridge anchorage while new urban transects
connect surrounding neighborhoods.

A sequence of new terraced greens create
links between street level pedestrian
routes and the higher level plazas of
the municipal buildings. New public spaces
for rest and recreation are created along
the parklike routes.

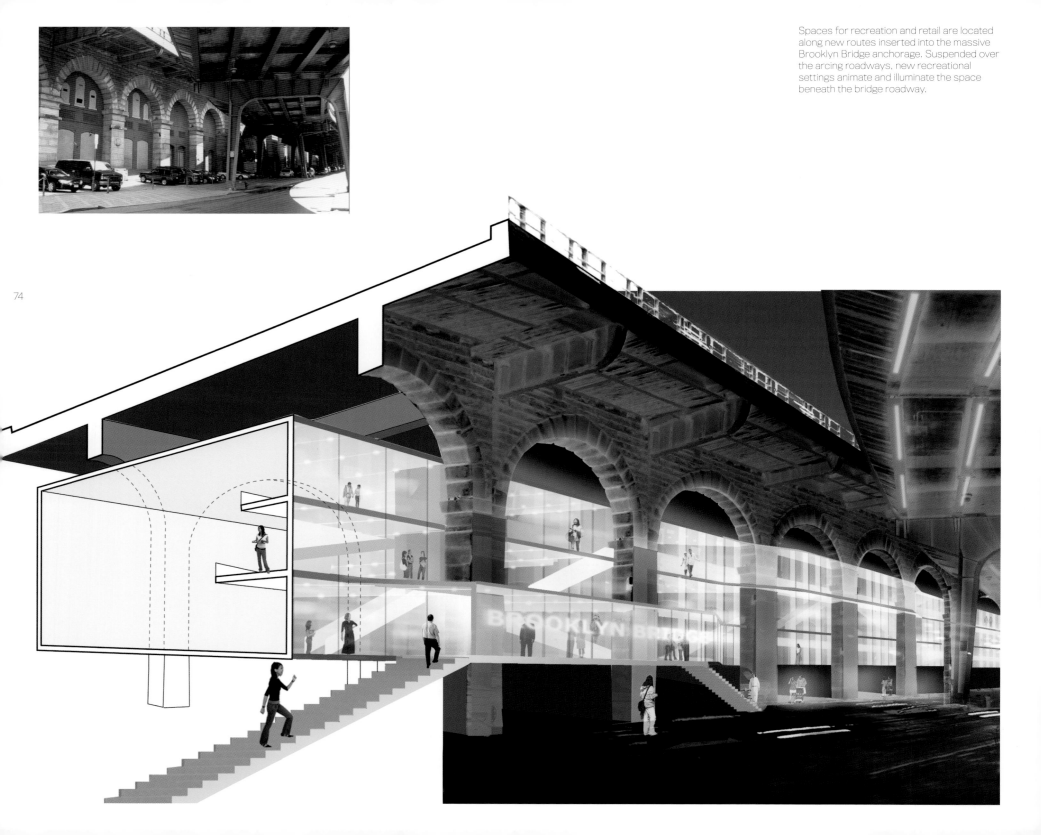

Spaces for recreation and retail are located along new routes inserted into the massive Brooklyn Bridge anchorage. Suspended over the arcing roadways, new recreational settings animate and illuminate the space beneath the bridge roadway.

INH
TOPOGRA
CU
EXCAVA

ABITING
PHIES:
LTIVATION/
ION

CONVERSATION
DETLEF MERTINS
MARION WEISS
MICHAEL MANFREDI

Detlef Mertins: Your projects seem to have been informed by the work of land artists as well as landscape architects. This seems to be the case not only with the urban scale projects but also smaller buildings such as the Museum of the Earth, the Brooklyn Botanic Garden, and the International Retreat. How does your interest in inhabiting topography relate to the shift in art practices in the 1960s from galleries into landscapes and urban spaces?

Marion Weiss: There are several compelling things about the movement of land art. Those artists discovered that figurative sculpture could leap off its pedestal directly into the space people occupy, first in the gallery and then in the landscape (Donald Judd, Richard Serra, Michael Heizer, Robert Smithson, Mary Miss). They recognized that their work could get off the wall and out of the galleries and locate itself into something larger. Land and the dialectics of nature and culture were the next terrain to engage. I admire the capacity of some land art to bring into focus that which is unseen. By imposing constructions of such clarity into unclear zones, they make you see things in a different way, whether it is the meter of a lightning field by Walter De Maria or the incisive cuts of Michael Heizer into the desert. The clarity of those shadows against the roughened surface made you see things you had not seen before on that very ground.

We're often very excited about the larger terrains that we operate in, like the Museum of the Earth, which has a six-acre site. The brief was to design a building, but for us it was also about how we could make evident the geologic forces that

shaped the glacial landscape of Ithaca. We wanted to do that through interventions with the landscape, whether through a series of water collecting parking terraces or embedded buildings. Our interest was to make present things that were latent, and I think that land art often reveals latent conditions in a site.

Michael Manfredi: It's been very interesting for us to work with artists like Richard Serra, Mark Dion, and Teresita Fernandez for the Olympic Sculpture Park and to see how they see their work in relation to nature, culture, and technology. Whereas Heizer often placed his work in the desert, a pure "nature" uncontaminated by the messy realities of culture and economic condition, Dion's work is about culture and nature and the intertwining of those two worlds. Both extremes are relevant in our own work particularly in the Olympic Sculpture Park.

DM: Why did you title your book Surface/Subsurface?

MM: We felt it imperative to pair surface with subsurface to avoid the implication that we were just interested in a skin. We wanted to confound the distinction between the surface and the subsurface. The idea of surface/subsurface implies something on the vertical, as opposed to the convention that ground is fundamentally horizontal. We are interested in the idea that something might be spongy, in a literal as well as a metaphoric way, and that sponginess might have certain richness.

DM: The idea that surface foregrounds a two-dimensional, extensive, and visible condition while subsurface alludes to the three-dimensionality of ground, which is

deep, intensive, and lends itself to cutting, filling, and exposing. Surface also suggests something more abstract and geometric than subsurface, which is material and massive but also energetic and charged with hidden forces.

MW: I think that's why the conflation of surface/subsurface is essential. The language of the surface in our projects tends to emerge from a set of under-standings about the subsurface, not just the physical subsurface, which is obvious, but also the cultural and social subsurface, which leads to interpreting or hybridizing programs and agendas. In the end all we see is the surface, but we want to also sense the subsurface in the work. For instance on the skin of the Barnard building, the surface is pretty important. While the surface of glass tends to be associated with slickness and reflectivity, in the Nexus, we etch the surface of the terracotta-colored glass to create a collaboration with the brick campus without resorting to a contextual imitation of the surrounding buildings.

DM: What's an example of a subsurface?

MM: Subsurface carries with it an infrastructural idea. What happens below the surface provides a chore-ography, a script, or it provides the nourishment, in a vascular way, for what we see on the surface. Just as the surface, when it's an interesting surface isn't something you can just peel away like the skin of an orange. It's embedded and becomes interesting formally and operationally.

Geologic or geotechnical engineers talk first about subsurface conditions. In some ways, they are the most interesting group

to talk to. In our project in Washington (the Women's Memorial), we were concerned about the water table. Our geotechnical engineer, James Gould, showed us how the Arlington Cemetery was at the intersection of the Potomac Alluvial Plain and the Piedmont Mountain Range. Initially, we just asked, is there water on the site? But all of a sudden, he launched into a revelatory dissertation on geologic forces and how in real terms they would affect the geometries of the design and the material conditions of the project.

DM: Is the term subsurface used for oceans as well as land?

MM: With oceans, we can certainly talk about subsurface or bathymetric conditions. If you're talking about a tsunami, you must first look at how waves multiply and reflect off the particular shape and depth of the ocean floor.

MW: An understanding of the subsurface condition can lead to a very different idea of what the surface manifestation is. For instance, the Arlington Cemetery site turned out to be effectively under water. That led to developing a concrete diaphragm, almost a doughnut, with a double wall to simultaneously water-proof and structure the building. Our first design that was structured in steel would have required a whole other set of structures to be built around it to deal with the water, so the subsurface condition generated a comprehensive structural form that performed in two ways rather than one.

The other issue is capacity. A subsurface capacity is not just physical but also

metaphorical. What's latent in a project—what's behind it—also has to do with its cultural history. The programmatic capacities or expectations of the subsurface lead to the form and the surface of form that we finally see. We are interested in the systemic conditions that are physical, cultural, programmatic, financial, and economic and reside in an unseen state but ultimately inform a project's form, which is reflected in the surface. Those conditions are potent for our work and tend to drive it.

DM: To what extent are the ecological aspects of landscape important to you? To what extent are growth over time, becoming overgrown, or even decaying important?

MM: They're extremely interesting aspects to our work. The issue of change, which is something fundamental to landscape, is increasingly relevant, not in the sense that change is in and of itself good in an architectural discussion, but because it implies a sense of humility. We realize that within the context of geologic time and climate change architectural projects are insignificant. Longer climactic and shorter seasonal cycles operate dramatically on how a project behaves. If you give into these cycles, they can actually enrich your work. Why resist them? Topography, topology, and change are formative in our work.

Both Marion and I came out of an architec-tural discussion of urban context in the '80s, which we thought had become limiting and frustrating. We found something interesting about seeing the landscape in a much larger and more dynamic kind of context. When you deal

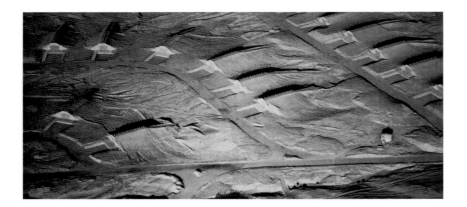

with landscape, or when you start to see architecture dissolve into landscape and vice versa, you start to think about time in its most elemental state. You think about geologic time, as well as the particulars of how the sun moves over the course of the day. That range of time frames and the active dimensions of landscape have actually provided a liberating set of realities. We realized that we didn't need to try to control every surface and freeze it in time. One starts to think about an architecture that takes a set of parameters, climatic and seasonal, and develops a rigorous idea of what those parameters are spatially, and then lets them play out. It's infrastructural in the way that landscapes can be understood as infrastructures within which natural processes occur.

DM: Your critique of modernist architecture as objects out of context makes me think of Alvar Aalto, who already reacted to the same concerns and started to borrow from landform and landscape in his architecture. He even decomposed the form of some of his buildings so that they were not single iconic objects but aggregates that integrated their sites and landforms and sometimes emulated topography. And he chose materials that would weather and wear beautifully over time. Would you say your work shares anything with Aalto's?

MM: Actually Aalto is a point of reference. He remains an increasingly relevant figure from the great modernist tradition. The town hall at Saynatsalo, which has a hill-like form, suggests topography and grows out of the ground as much as it melts into it. Aalto is very relevant for us in terms of the idea of topography, and I think his anticipation of weathering

and the dissolve between building and site are important to our work.

DM: Would you say that your buildings dissolve more?

MM: To the extent that we hope one would have a hard time discerning where the building stops and the landscape begins; our buildings vary in their degree of merging with or emerging from their sites.

DM: Would you say that Frank Lloyd Wright did something similar at Taliesin or other projects of his?

MM: Wright is in some ways more assertive than Aalto. Wright's work, on the one hand, presents itself as camouflage but then very quickly reasserts itself. That's the great paradox of Fallingwater, which appears to be about nature but it's not. That particular project, because of the tension, is, for us, extraordinarily interesting, refreshing, and something we return to.

MW: In fact Fallingwater was an inspiration early on. I remember going through books on art and architecture when I was young and being fascinated by the black and white pictures of Fallingwater; the drama of the waterfall was given presence by the cantilevering planes of the architecture—the waterfall, in turn, made the architecture all the more remarkable.

MW: Topography describes a surface that changes and inhabitation talks about its occupation. I'm fascinated by the chameleon as an entity that not only can come, show up, transform itself to be a part of the setting but also can transform

the setting by its occupation. All of our projects have an agenda of collaboration with the setting, radically transforming it to allow us to see different things. Because they are architecture they inhabit the setting. At the Museum of the Earth a series of berms organize and channel water as well as simultaneously conceal the parking of cars, which are a huge and difficult obligation for any museum. The berms, which camouflage the visitors' cars, also choreograph water into the operative organizing force for the landscape and the architecture.

DM: Your transformations of the land establish new geometries in the way that some earthworks did.

MW: What is intriguing about Michael Heiser's cuts in the dessert is that they make us wonder about their scale, geometry, and depth.

The other important thing to stress is that in addition to a geometric operation there's also an performative operation. While the Museum of the Earth marks the scale of the site and certain geologic processes, what is interesting operationally is the channeling of water and allowing the visitor to understand the role water plays in shaping the environment.

DM: Are there similar issues at work in your visitor center for the Brooklyn Botanic Garden?

MM: Yes, there are. Since it's a work in progress we are still trying to test out certain opportunities. The building shifts from a free-standing building at the edge of the city into an arc of glass embedded into the landscape at the center of the botanic garden. While we are using the earth as both insulation and source for a geothermal system, we are also using it as a material that shifts from a base for building into a surrounding material. We are currently thinking about what it might mean to plant a roof in such a way that it transcends the cliché signature of green building. We want to make sure that it demonstrates the temporal characteristics of growth, supporting the Botanic Garden's commitment to showing how different things grow and how different cycles operate.

MW: In the botanic garden we are literally incising a volume into that topography that can be inhabited. It's partly covered by a landscape and partly covered by a building. The building is a hybrid; at first glance it is highly architectural and urban and then shifts to be camouflaged in the hillside itself. We're reinvigorating the architecture with an agenda of landscape, but we're also questioning the system of the botanic garden, which is an inventory of landscapes that are intensified for enjoyment. We're not interested in camouflaging the building completely but want the building to assert itself at the city's edge and then establish a new interface between landscape and architecture.

MW: For us there is a difference between seeing the landscape as a passive picturesque background for buildings and seeing it as teaming with dynamic processes, activities, and behaviors with which buildings interact. We like to think that these phenomena can, in fact, be formative for the design of our work. Perhaps

we need to see the making of buildings as not that far removed from the agricultural model of cultivation—of managing land and water systematically for productive effects.

For the Olympic Sculpture Park in Seattle and the Museum of the Earth in Ithaca we explored the way water was at play and tested how to keep it in play after we had rebuilt the sites. Municipalities now oblige new buildings to retain rainwater on their sites. Most often it's held in the subsurface, which means we never see it. It ended up being both less expensive and far more interesting to allow the collecting and cleansing of water to be part of the formal making of those landscapes. At the Museum of the Earth, the site works and the earth berms we made were largely conceived as legible water management strategies. While buildings go to great lengths to keep the water out, landscape goes to great lengths to recognize that water is part of being of the world. That's true also at our park in Seattle, where our design collects water. There, storm water is captured on the site, collected through a series of pipes and tubes, and released to nourish planting in the prebeach area. The collection and cultivation of water is tied into the artifice and infrastructure of the park's artificial landscape.

DM: Does thinking of the building as a topography help you spatialize its program of uses and activities, in planning how life is going to take place in it?

MM: We operate intuitively, by looking and thinking in terms of shaping sequences and developing sectionally rich space. If you bring those two things together,

you get the idea of topography, which reveals a spatial experience through time and movement. The idea of topography is particularly relevant not only as a metaphor for working but also for developing sets of spaces that have a cinematic quality and sectional richness.

The International Retreat did not provide much topography to work with, so we thought in terms of adding and removing, to open up views and sequences that would engage the larger context of the estate. By taking out the center of that set of buildings and introducing a series of quadrants with views, movements, and connections into the surrounding landscape, we transformed a relatively flat building site into a more expansive and topographically rich condition.

THE MUSEUM OF THE EARTH
ITHACA, NEW YORK

The Museum of the Earth, commissioned by the Paleontological Research Institution, engages the remarkable landforms of the state's Finger Lakes region. The museum houses one of the nation's largest paleontological collections and demonstrates the intrinsic relationships between geological events and biological evolution. Shifted and carved by a receding ice sheet twenty thousand years ago, the site is marked by a gradual, forty-foot slope. The design capitalizes on this rich condition, making vivid the dynamic interrelationship between biology and geology that is central to the museum's mission.

Approached from the south, a series of sculpted landforms and linear water terraces organize the site and museum into a coherent whole. These ten-foot-high landscaped berms, which recall moraines, define and conceal four distinct parking areas. Precisely graded, the parking areas divert groundwater runoff to bioswales with gravel filters and reintroduced prehistoric grasses such as equisetum, cleansing the groundwater of chemicals and other pollutants. Channelled into the linear-stepped and stone-lined terrace, water is directed between the two museum wings, where it collects in a reflecting pool. Excess water fills the pool until it overflows into a new wetlands detention basin that calibrates the release of water into nearby Lake Cayuga.

Set into the hillside and adjacent to the existing research facility, the museum is organized into two parallel buildings—a public education wing and an exhibition wing—that are connected below grade. These structures are defined by a series of cast-in-place concrete walls, aluminum curtain walls, and standing-seam copper roofs cantilevered over the two wings of the museum. The partially buried structures define the edges of a cascading plaza, extending views to the lake and the surrounding landscape.

The twenty thousand square-foot museum is organized in section to capitalize on the change of grade and provide a varied and spatially rich itinerary for the museum visitor. Just inside the exhibition hall entrance, the lobby takes the form of a bridge leading to a reception area and gift shop. To the left of the bridge, the complete skeleton of a rare Right whale, a contemporary mammal, is suspended above the exhibition area, which is reached by a long ramp. As visitors walk along the ramp they descend in time, passing artist Barbara Page's installation of 543 different panels, each representing one million years of geologic history. On the lower level, the exhibition extends through three geological periods, Devonian, Triassic, and Quaternary; interactive exhibits with more than 650 specimens are on view, including the ancient skeleton of a woolly mammoth.

In addition to innovative water-management strategies, a number of other sustainable initiatives support the pedagogic mission of the museum. The below-grade exhibition hall benefits from thermal insulation achieved by embedding both wings of the complex deep within the earth. Heating and cooling systems for the building are supplemented by geothermal energy provided by two ground-source water pumps that harness energy from fifteen hundred feet beneath the earth's surface. This energy is transformed into radiant floor heating in the winter and fed into an air-handling system for heating and cooling year round.

The design of the Museum of the Earth capitalizes on ideas of entropy-sedimentation, erosion, and freeze/thaw cycles—that relate to the glacially gouged topography unique to the Finger Lakes region. Rather than considering the site as distinct and separate from the museum, this project creates a new topography: a continuous, terraced landscape that fuses architecture and ecology into a cohesive expression of the geologic processes involved in the region's formation.

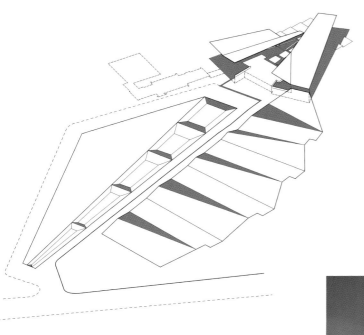

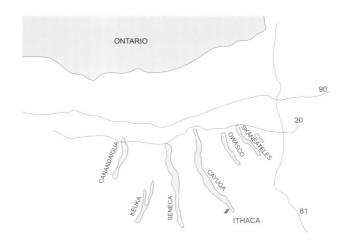

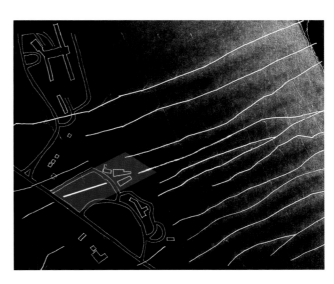

In upstate New York, the retreating Wisconsin-era glacier left deep gouges in the earth's surface that have become the dramatic Finger Lakes. Water cascades to the lakes through long and straight gorges cleaved in the hills. Sections of ancient sediments are revealed in strata of local siltstone. These dynamic geologic forces expose the preserved fossil record of the region.

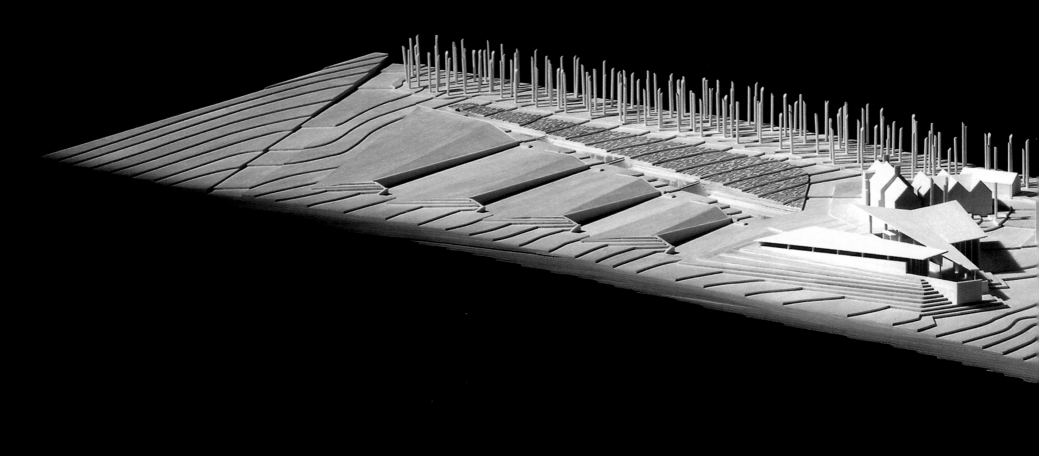

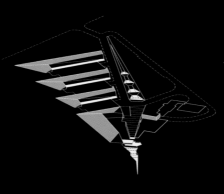

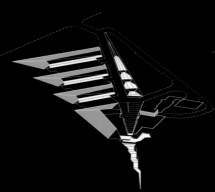

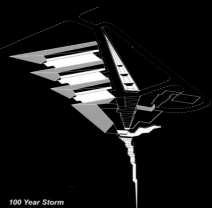

10 Year Storm
7,616 c.f. of water

50 Year Storm
12,913 c.f. of water

100 Year Storm
15,221 c.f. of water

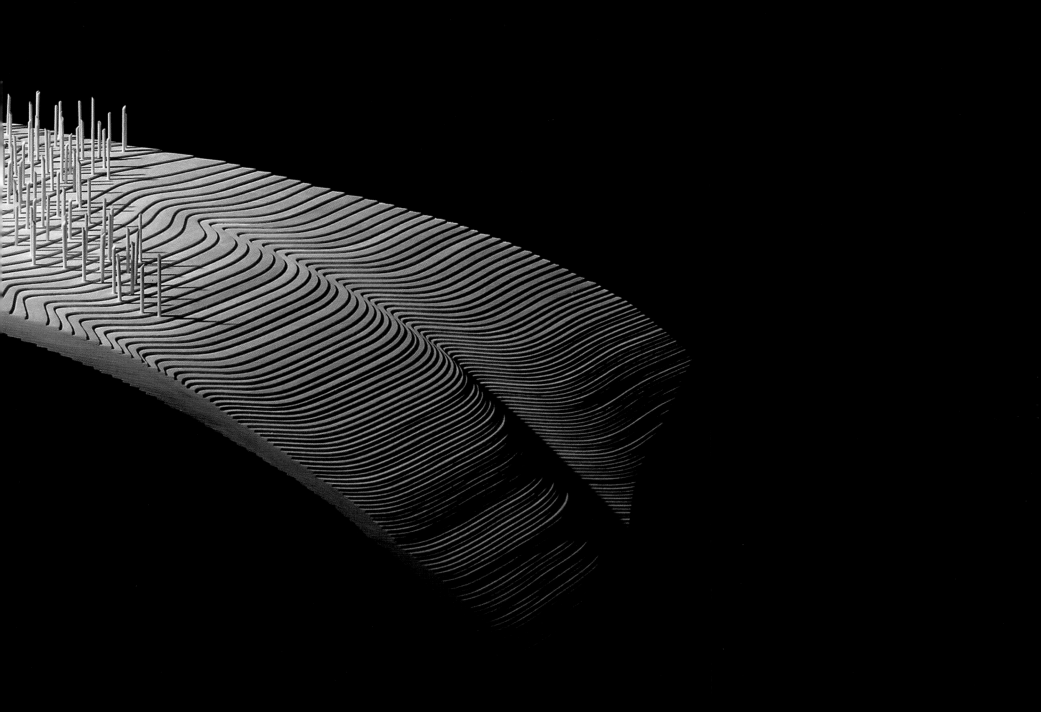

As visitors enter the museum they are greeted by the skeleton of a right whale. Visitors then descend a ramp passing a sequence of 543 painted panels by artist Barbara Page, each depicting a million years of geologic time. At the base of the ramp, visitors encounter the oldest rock in the museum's collection before entering the exhibition galleries. This descending route allows visitors to trace their journey back in time.

The two museum pavilions define a descending central courtyard, which recalls the spatial condition of many of Ithaca's dramatic gorges. A below-grade passage links the entrance pavilion to the exhibition pavilion. The concrete in the central court is left deliberately raw to make vivid its material presence and formation.

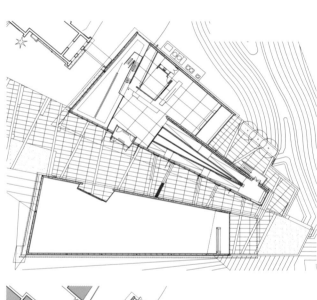

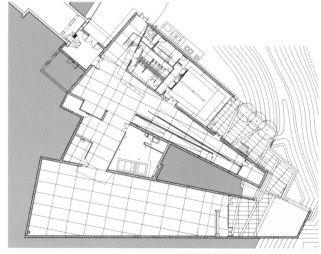

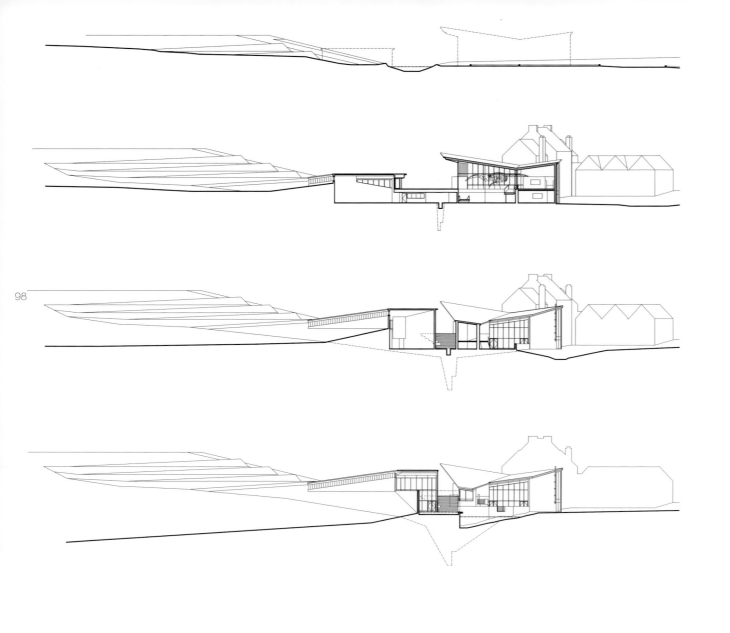

BROOKLYN BOTANIC GARDEN VISITOR CENTER
BROOKLYN, NEW YORK

A botanic garden is an unusual kind of museum, a fragile collection constantly in flux. As a constructed "natural" environment, it is dependent on man made infrastructures to thrive. New York City's Brooklyn Botanic Garden contains a wide variety of landscapes organized into discrete settings such as the Japanese Garden, the Cherry Esplanade, the Osborne Garden, the Overlook, and the Cranford Rose Garden. The Botanic Garden exists as an oasis in the city, visually separated from the neighborhood by elevated berms and trees.

To provoke curiosity and interest in its world-class collection, the Brooklyn Botanic Garden visitor center provides a legible point of arrival and orientation, an interface between garden and city, culture and cultivation. The building is conceived as an inhabitable topography that defines a new threshold between the city and the constructed landscapes of the fifty-two acre garden.

Sited at Washington Avenue and within the berm that separates the Brooklyn Museum parking lot from the botanic garden, the visitor center provides clear orientation and access to the major garden precincts such as the Japanese Garden and the Cherry Esplanade. The center includes an exhibition gallery, information lobby, orientation room, gift shop, café, and an events space.

Like the gardens themselves, the building is experienced cinematically and is never seen in its entirety. The serpentine form of the visitor center is generated by the garden's existing pathways. The primary entry to the building from Washington Avenue is visible from the street and a

secondary route from the top of the berm slides through the visitor center, frames views of the Japanese garden, and descends through a stepped ramp to the main level of the garden.

The curved glass walls of the center's gallery are a mediating surface between the building and the landscape. The fritted surfaces of the glass filter light and provide veiled views into the garden. By contrast, the north side of the center is inscribed into the berm. The steel framed superstructure adjusts to the curved plan and gives shape to the undulating roof canopy. The building utilizes earth mass and spectrally selective fritted glass to achieve a high-performing building envelope, minimizing heat gain and maximizing natural illumination. A geothermal heat-exchange system is used to heat and cool the interior spaces. Additional sustainable strategies include a green roof, stormwater management, and rainwater collection that irrigate a series of landscaped terraces.

A chameleon-like structure, the visitor center transitions from an architectural presence at the street into a structured landscape in the botanic garden. This center redefines the physical and philosophical relationship between visitor and garden, introducing new connections between landscape and structure, exhibition and movement.

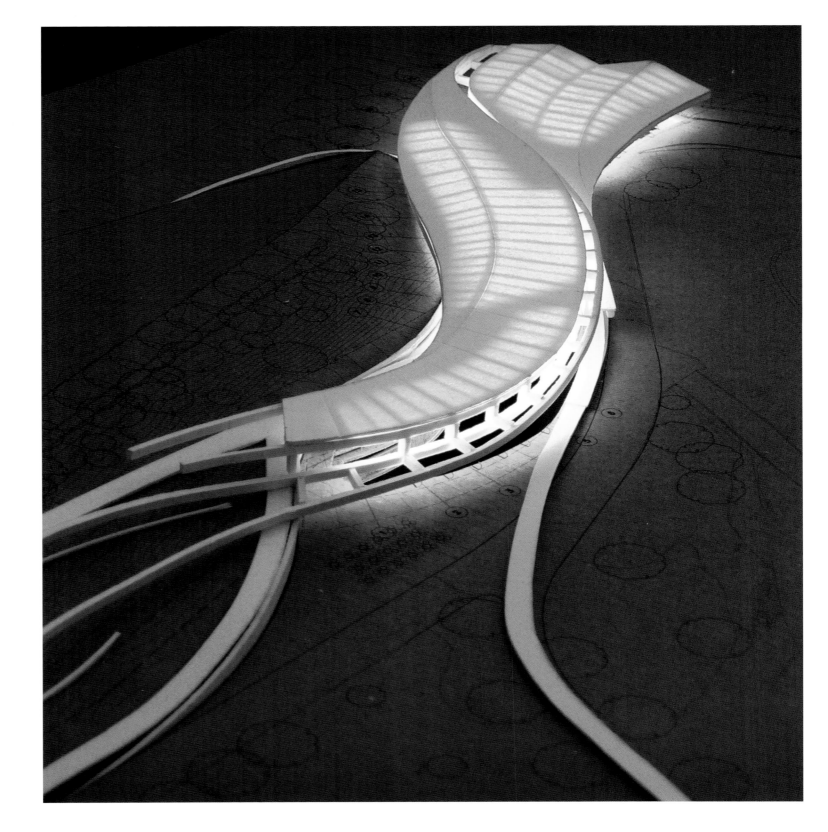

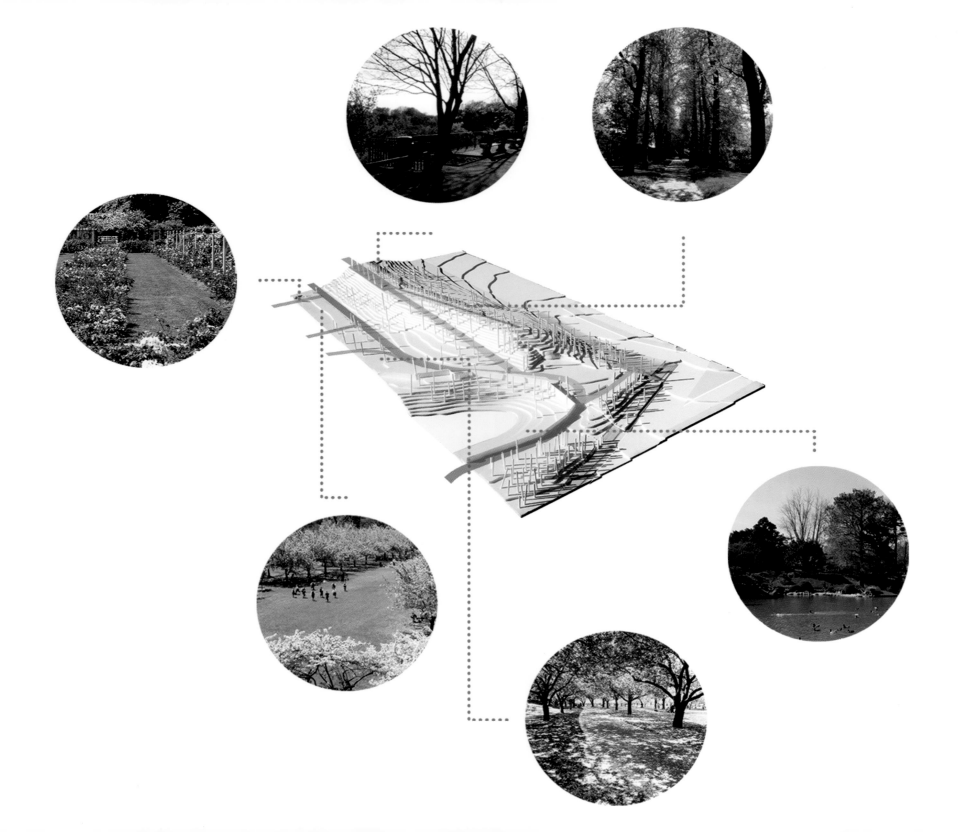

The Brooklyn Botanic Garden connects
a collection of garden types, including
a traditional rose garden, a restored
forest, a formal cherry esplanade,
and a Japanese garden. The topography
of the site informs the architectural
development of the visitor center through
a sequence of distinct garden settings.

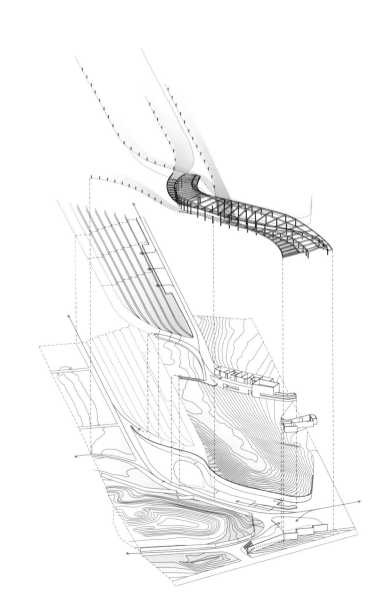

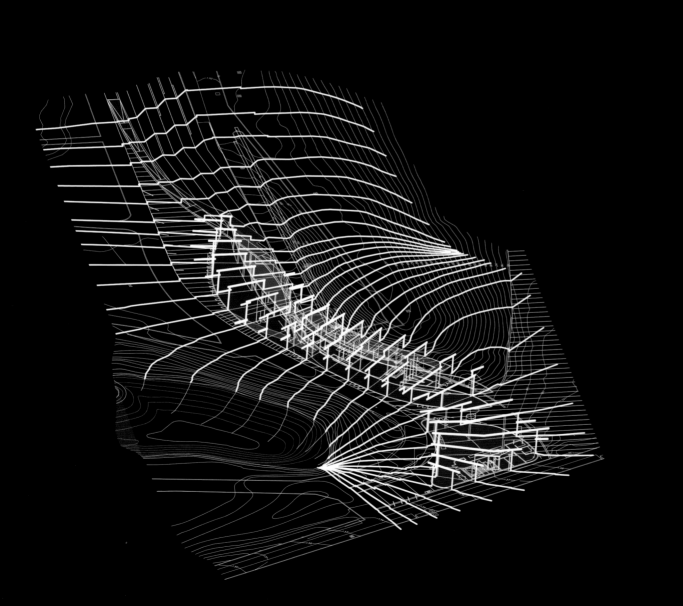

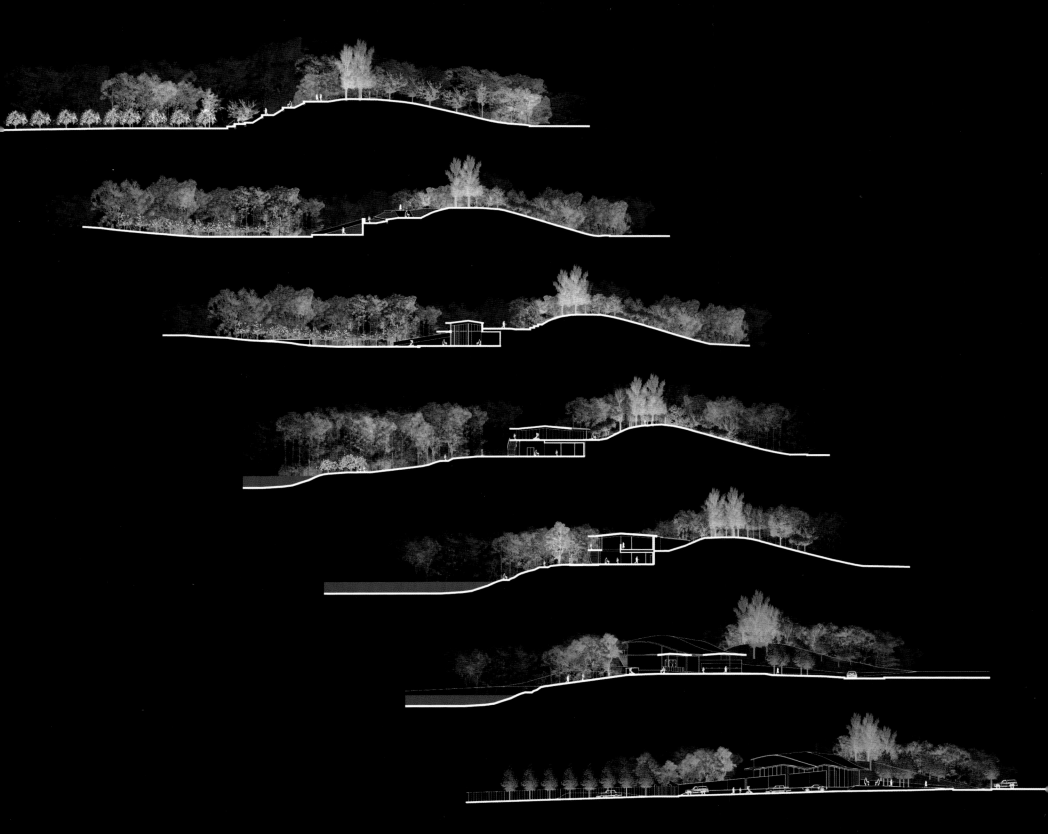

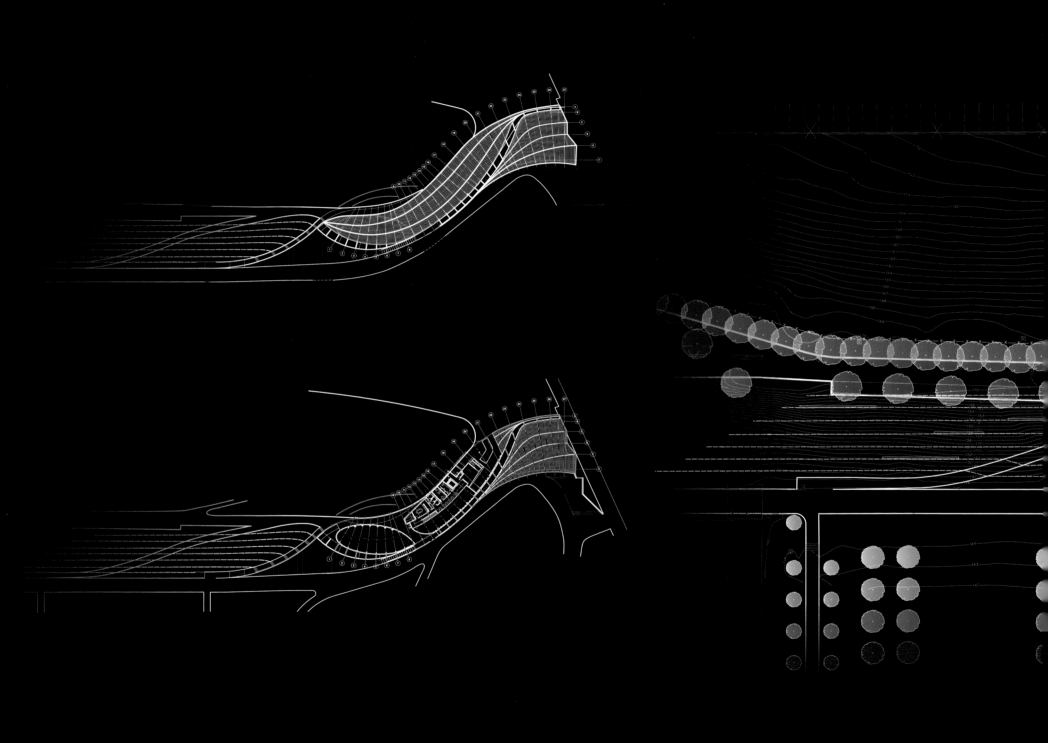

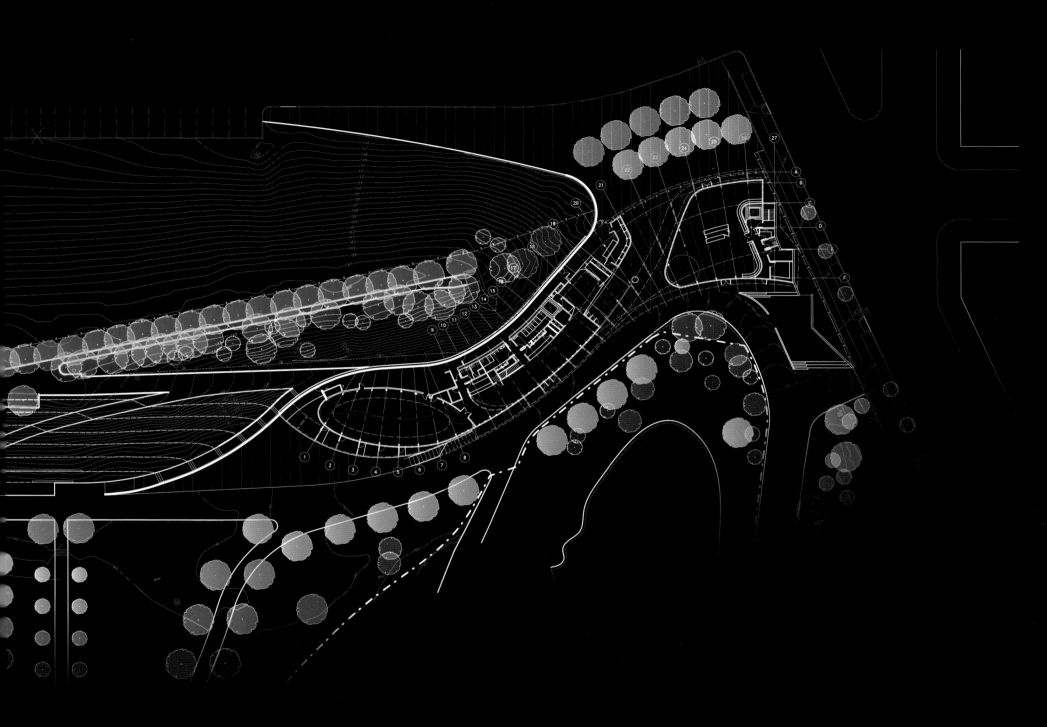

A canopy shelters the main entry route to the visitor center. This route wanders through the building and connects to an upper level garden path. Views of and into the garden are alternately hidden and revealed.

INTERNATIONAL RETREAT

Cultivation, a word that is associated with the productive transformation of the land, can also be understood as the root of diplomacy. The dual understanding of this word informed the design of this international retreat, a high level conference center created for international organizations to discuss global justice, human rights, and world economic policy. Located on a verdant four hundred-acre site, the retreat transforms a collection of early twentieth-century structures—including a boarding house, horse stable, and garage—into a hybrid assemblage of landscape and architecture.

Two intersecting landscapes, organized into four gardens, are inscribed into the existing collection of buildings, creating a framework for connecting the renovated and programmatically transformed structures. At the center of these landscapes, a new gallery wing replaces the existing boarding house and creates a focus for the informal gatherings that are as essential as the formal meetings that take place at the retreat.

The north-south landscape is defined by an unbounded linear organization of water, trees, crushed stone, and flowering ground cover. A linear reflecting pool at the north end provides a formal environment for arrival; a more informal setting of water, trees, and outdoor seating defines the south garden. The east-west landscape links the renovated garage and stables, capturing residual exterior spaces and turning them into cultivated gardens. A distinct nine-foot module organizes water and landscape as well as the gallery structure that resides at the intersection of these two landscapes.

The interior and exterior programs intersect at the elliptically shaped glazed gallery, which is envisioned as an informal setting to encourage the spontaneous encounters that often initiate significant discussions among visitors. This double-height space, rendered in steel and glass, is at the heart of the conference center complex and opens to the four gardens. Located between the formal conference center, which occupies the renovated garage, and the guest room wing, located in the renovated stables, the gallery unites all the events that occur over the course of a conference.

As much a part of the landscape as it is a part of the building complex, the gallery, taking cues from the existing conservatory structures located on the former estate, houses both real and artificial landscapes. Long-leaved ficus trees shade a carpet of green wool, which, in its thirty-six shades, emulates the mowing patterns seen on the surrounding hills of the property. The elliptical gallery structure, which replaces the old boarding house, was engineered and fabricated in Germany; its custom-fritted glass modulates and tempers natural light from above and from the south. An exhibition space and library overlook the gallery and feature selected works from the historic estate's collection of art, books, and historic correspondence.

In contrast to the transparent gallery, the main conference room is internally focused, illuminated by an existing skylight. A series of overlapping wood wall panels with laser-cut perforations are calibrated to ensure acoustically balanced sound distribution throughout the room. The wood wall, which also accommodates extensive power and teledata requirements, mediates the scale of the white tile-clad garage and the elliptically shaped conference room table.

To accommodate varying degrees of enclosure and openness, the International Retreat creates opportunities for focused discussions as well as informal conversations. Glass, steel, water, and extensive landscaping, produce a layered set of relationships among the renovated existing buildings, new structures, and grounds, removing boundaries between interior and exterior spaces. The year-round retreat provides a setting for the cultivation of relationships essential to creating international peace.

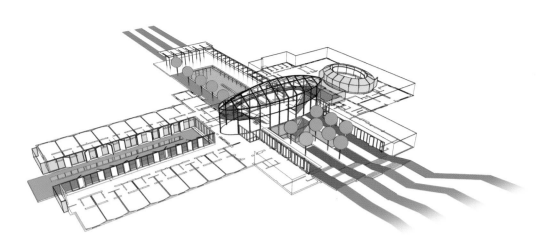

The existing boarding house is transformed by water and glass into a light filled connection between the renovated garage and stables.

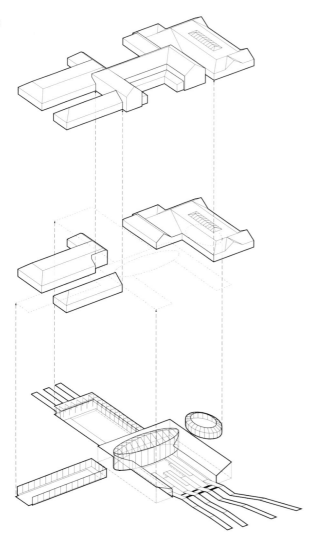

A luminous reflecting pool marks the north entry courtyard, passes under the glazed gallery, and connects to an informal water garden at the south courtyard.

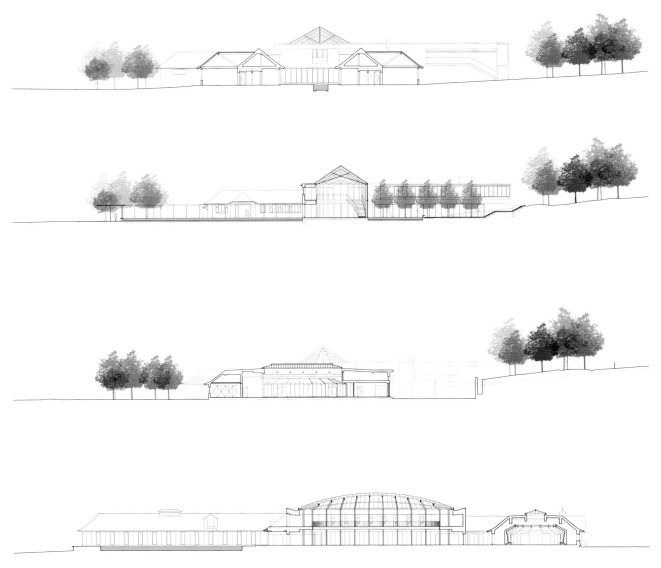

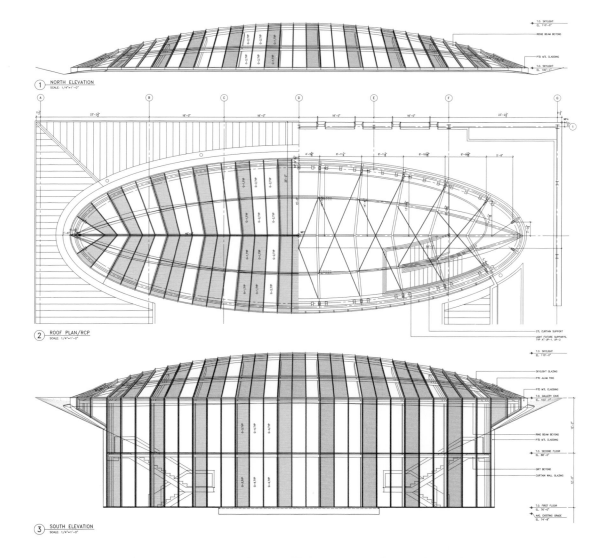

① NORTH ELEVATION
SCALE: 1/4"=1'-0"

② ROOF PLAN/RCP
SCALE: 1/4"=1'-0"

③ SOUTH ELEVATION
SCALE: 1/4"=1'-0"

The skeletal steel structure was fabricated,
tested, and preassembled in Germany.
The one hundred ten-foot-long elliptical gallery
is comprised of a series of prewelded tubular
columns and trusses tensioned through
a system of alternating stainless-steel rods.
The glass envelope is a combination of clear
and fritted low-iron glass from Austria.

The gallery, conceived as a conservatory structure located at the intersection of two crossing gardens, includes indoor plantings and a custom designed rug. Woven with thirty-six shades of wool to provide an almost infinite gradient of color, the rug emulates the mowing patterns of the estate's adjacent fields.

The wood elliptical enclosure of the formal conference room is inserted within the volume of a former garage. The garage's original surfaces and skylights have been restored. Interlocking cherry wood panels are cantilevered from the floor and are perforated for optimal acoustic performance.

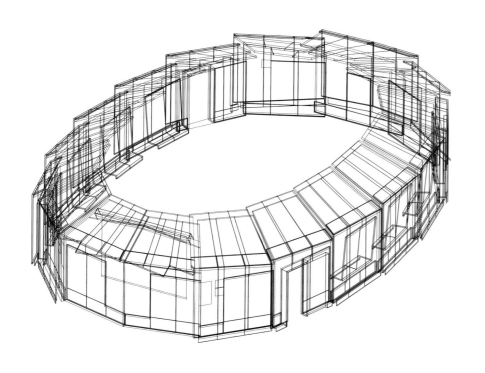

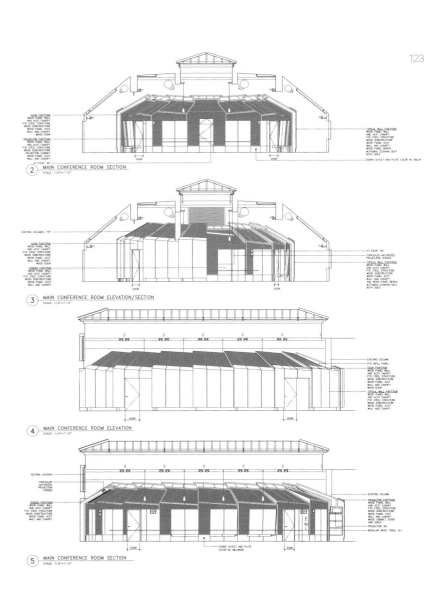

2 MAIN CONFERENCE ROOM SECTION
SCALE: 1/4"=1'-0"

3 MAIN CONFERENCE ROOM ELEVATION/SECTION
SCALE: 1/4"=1'-0"

4 MAIN CONFERENCE ROOM ELEVATION
SCALE: 1/4"=1'-0"

5 MAIN CONFERENCE ROOM SECTION
SCALE: 1/4"=1'-0"

Interior and exterior landscapes are linked via a series of framed vistas. A three-foot module, a recurring dimension in the existing buildings, is used to organize all the new interventions, including the structural system of the gallery and the landscape elements in the gardens.

LEVERAGI
M
PERIPHE
VISION

NG
OVEMENT:
RAL

CONVERSATION
DETLEF MERTINS
MARION WEISS
MICHAEL MANFREDI

Detlef Mertins: Movements of different kinds are, of course, integral to both the infrastructures and landscapes that we've already talked about: the movement of cars, trains, bicycles, and people, of water, glaciers, and energy. Interestingly enough, movement was also seen as formative for many modernist architects who sought to engage the dynamics of the metropolis, like Le Corbusier and Team X, or to integrate building and landscape, like Wright, Aalto, and later Carlo Scarpa. While Le Corbusier retained the opposition of architecture and nature, he also brought the experience of moving through a landscape or along a highway into his buildings in the form of the "architectural promenade."

Michael Manfredi: In fact, a promenade is by definition a walk. It implies moving through space and across a surface, up and down. These are conditions that prioritize the sectional development of a project and foreground its topography. It would be fair to say that for us the architectural promenade has a strong connection to the idea of landscape and specifically to topography.

DM: How is orchestrating movement, vision, and experience formative for your projects and specifically for their public spaces? How do you leverage movement and visual experience in projects like the Smith College Campus Center, the Robin Hood Library, and the Barnard Nexus in Manhattan?

Marion Weiss: With Smith and Barnard, both private institutions, we've been preoccupied with their public life. At Barnard, by drawing together the library, café, and critique spaces through a series of visually linked atria, these spaces create interaction and public life within the building. This condition, found on the Broadway side of the building, creates a signature of the intellectual and social life of the school—a public face to the city. But the simplicity of this visually linked section has a radical counterpoint—the west stair wanders on the opposite side, creating a seemingly random relationship to these public spaces, encouraging offhand and spontaneous encounters as students move through the building.

MM: There's a definite preoccupation on our part to invite people in. At Smith, the college recognized that the building was a part of the city and the linear, wandering, triple-level, occupiable path we designed was a public route as well as a place for students and the community in Northampton, Massachusetts. The Olmsted designed campus included a highly layered landscape of paths. These routes held the campus together in a way its buildings did not. Even the shortcut path that had wandered through our site's existing parking lot joined the network of Olmsted's paths. What Olmsted's plan didn't anticipate was the potential of a more labyrinthian and sectionally dynamic network of paths that might link three levels of public life in one location. What became central for us was establishing this new connective tissue to support a super-public life, encouraging an open exchange between people en route between academic spaces and residential spaces. We wanted our building to embody the sense of discovery that, ideally, academic institutions should support.

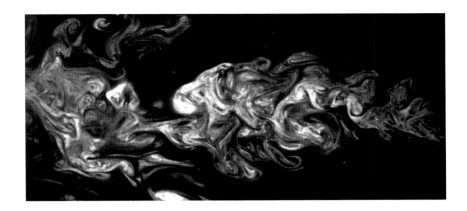

DM: Adding another level is an example of what you mean when you say leveraging movement.

MW: That became the impetus of the project—intensifying the Olmsted path by making it richer in section. Its intertwining multilevel section heightens the viewer's attention and invites both vertical and lateral peripheral vision. We're not just interested in what you see but who you see above you, below you, and passing in different directions on stairs and bridges. We take a horizontal landscape path and leverage it to create a new experience within the building. We exploited the confluence of traffic that marks it as a place where people meet.

DM: Tell me more about the peripheral aspect of the visual experiences your buildings create.

MW: Our experiences are formed by the things that catch the corner of our eye and stimulate inquiries that otherwise wouldn't occur. The cubist collages of Picasso and Braque and more recent work by video artists allow us to simultaneously read the front, side, top, and bottom of a particular subject. The effect of reading these collages is one of interpreting a condensed recording of what a peripheral scan might reveal, but the conflation of these views suggest an entirely different interpretation of the subject at hand. For a mixed-use building, especially, we want to capitalize on the potential effect of peripheral vision to bring forth cross-fertilization between programmatically distinct and separate spaces. In a building designed to foster public engagement, this stimulation, this

distraction, is essential to encourage new social and intellectual hybrid spaces.

MM: In Seattle, for example, even though there's a clear primary route, there are also ways for the nonconformist, the anarchists, to veer off-path. That's another aspect of peripheral vision: we're not interested in prescribing or programming the experience so tightly that it precludes the experiential frictions that give us all pleasure. In Seattle you can see a tractor trailer pull up next to Mark Dion's environmental sculpture, which is an unexpected and extreme juxtaposition of activities. These sorts of contrasts are highlighted by the proximity of multiple programs and often occur in surprising and unpredictable ways. We like to encourage multiple strands of movement that offer programmatic opportunities that are improvisational and aren't so strongly choreographed by the architect.

DM: Would you say that all your projects are routes?

MM: I think they are, actually. The promenade is central to our work. This goes back to the issue of the ground, because the ground implies a route. I'm thinking Specchi's project for the Spanish Steps, which is a route—an extraordinary piece of infrastructure and public investment. It certainly deals with issues of topography, and it probably deals with issues that, to this day, resonate for disturbing the conventions of what's public and private. One can have an extraordinarily private encounter there in public, as well as a public encounter that might be privatized. The other project that we always return to is Gaudi's Park Guell, which is a route as

much as a place. It confounds the reading of what is surface and what is subsurface; it morphologically redefines the ground as structure and the structure as ground. Park Guell is an extraordinary piece of infrastructure, and like the Spanish Steps, it is a highly sensuous place, a pleasure to be in. For us, a project has to operate at a visceral as well as intellectual level. How you experience it, how you feel it, how your body moves through it: these all matter.

MW: The route, as a precinct of inhabiting movement and of peripheral vision, a loose-fit thread, is especially relevant for mixed-use programs, where we try to transcend the placing of one use here and another there. Engagement that occurs between these programs often occurs in the act of stepping out of a classroom or going out for coffee. Mixing uses and experiences is very much like the life of a city. A city is experienced en route. It's the distraction that a place offers that makes us want to return to it, to be a part of it. It's the sense of the detour and the things you see by turning this way or that, which we've tried to optimize in our projects. At Smith, the curvature encourages you to continue to see what's around the corner. A straight path places your destination on axis but reveals little of the distractions and detours along the way. In Seattle, the zigzag path structures a line of movement that unfolds to reveal distinctly different settings. In one direction it offers extraordinary views of the mountains and water, and in the other direction it offers a singular new view of the city and the port. Designing a route may appear offhand, but in fact the aspirations of what's included and what's excluded are highly specific.

MM: This takes us back to Le Corbusier's promenade architectural, to his Salvation Army building or his La Tourette monastery. La Tourette is always photographed as an object in the landscape but you approach it very differently; you go through a series of dense spatial experiences and the topography drops off. It's far richer in person and its episodic quality is still refreshing. The other project that we come back to is Mies's Barcelona Pavilion. The iconic textbook views are great, but what was a huge revelation to us were the little subtle changes of grade, the topographic qualities that can't be experienced from the photographs. It's a delicate construction with an extraordinarily high level of compression, expansion, light and dark, smooth and rough, and subtle ups and downs.

We often talk about the importance of nonprogrammed spaces. We're always fighting to reclaim that which isn't program. Often it is the place of movement, the route where different programs are given an opportunity to affect each other and come together.

MW: In our Whitney Center project, a new landscape carves through the collection of existing structures, creating connections between all of the three previously disconnected buildings. What emerged as the most important element was the place of greatest transition. The conservatory/gallery space, the intersection of crossings between the conference area and guest rooms, is given room to breathe, ultimately asserting its identity as an interior landscape—a place to pause between the intensity of meetings and the retreat of the guest rooms. It transcends the

limitations of efficient circulation and, instead, invites slowing down, joining a conversation, gazing into the garden. By giving it enough presence and, room to breathe, it's become recognized as the most special place there, when in fact it's just part of a circulation route. Often circulation spaces extend the limits of a site and the definition of useable space. Our client understood that, even though the gallery wasn't initially in their program, it could become the single most important space in the building. For many institutional clients, the efficiency of circulation and the ratio of net-to-gross floor area are taken to be a crucial benchmark of fiscal responsibility. But in our work, however, these circulation spaces often become the primary locus and identity of the building. They add value in countless ways. They are, in fact, extraordinarily efficient at meeting the most important goals and creating long-lasting value. Arguably the large volume of a church could be seen as the most egregious waste of space. I would argue that an efficient building might be the least compelling building of all because it considers fiscal responsibility in terms that are too narrow and shortsighted.

DM: This mobile sense of use and effect suggests another aspect of inhabiting space.

MW: With the Robin Hood Library we wanted to help a community and encourage reading. We made the books and the computer workstations the most provocative thing for students to see by placing them into an occupiable "bookworm" that weaves through the space. In it, the books and computers appear and disappear again. And children

can look through that wall like a construction fence; its perforations become reading windows. Everything rolls and moves in that project, from the bookshelves to the bean-bag chairs and curtains. We didn't want people to just park themselves in the library but to constantly explore it.

MM: In our building for Barnard, the mobility will come as different programs start to inhabit and move around the building. Eating and having coffee can occur in the library or in the studios, and doesn't necessarily need to be relegated only to the café, At PS 42, the principal believed as we did, that learning and playing were not mutually exclusive. By coincidence, the library transforms a former gym. It became apparent to us that the way children learn is through playing, which is antithetical to the convention of the quiet solitary scholar. So the idea of mobility—little groups of children could sit on chairs, move around, and go from a book to a computer and somehow not have to suppress their energy—was something that we tried to encourage architecturally. The sense of play, movement, and changeability that we associate with how children learn became important to the design.

DM: The library is a single space with differentiated areas within it, but you are always aware of all the other spaces regardless of where you happen to be, which is another way that you create peripheral experiences. There's a curtain that can be opened and closed to create a smaller more private space, but even it is still acoustically part of the larger room.

MW: Our intent was to create a setting that stimulates peripheral vision; a rich and optically tempting field. The first glance provides an immediate scan of one space, but multiple environments loosely held together by the wandering wall of books assert themselves at a second glance. In that sense, the library brings an intense and varied world to our immediate disposal. We like to create that kind of intensity and vibrancy in our work, whether it's for small intimate spaces within the library or the larger expanse of the entire space.

DM: By organizing many of your buildings around internal public routes, often on several levels at once, open to the outside, and undulating with the landform of their sites, you imbue them with a kind of animation in their physical fabric, too. Perhaps one could say that they are themselves dynamic, liquid, flowing like a stream. Do you see them that way? Are they a counterpoint to movement or in motion themselves?

MW: Our preoccupation with movement, topography, and continuities has paralleled our interest in the material presence of architecture. Arguably, the dynamic and fluid movement systems we promote reflects our interest in eradicating the line between public and private spaces. Yet in each of our projects, this interest is seen in parallel with material choices that often provide a modulating counterpoint to these continuities. At Barnard, the sensibility of sight, visual connections, and transparency translated into the material choice for the building exterior. The etching of the exterior surface created a soft rather than reflective finish, and by deploying gradients of this material from transparent

to translucent to opaque, we were able to selectively reveal and conceal the internal life of the building. The single line of the slipped gallery is the most transparent, while the studio spaces offer a range of transparent, translucent, and opaque surfaces. At Smith, the internal continuities of movement are marked by the meter of the interior wood panels that extend the language and rhythm of the white wood exterior battens. But this material choice which at first glance joins the campus's painted wood buildings, is translated into one that marks the meter of movement around and through the building with a syncopated pattern.

DM: The motion of people through buildings is, then, just one of many motions, although formative and key as is the mobility of uses. You spoke about water earlier, too, and even about the formation of the earth in geological time. We could add weather and the seasons as well. Do you see your architecture serving to situate people (viewing subjects) within fields, or landscapes, or universes of movement and interactivity? How inclusive is that universe? Why is it important for architecture to do this kind of work of situating, providing orientation, and facilitating relations among things and others?

MM: The ability to situate people, or more importantly the way in which people can situate themselves within fields or landscapes of movement, is of great interest to us. Movement that is too clear, too direct, is never very satisfying. We look for choreography of movement: there is a script but the participants are encouraged to improvise, to situate

themselves. In this sense we are very interested in dance as an analogous discipline and the tension between scripting and interpretation is a fertile territory for us. This creative tension is a reality even within the apparently restrictive and rigorous canon of classical ballet and is certainly exploited in contemporary dance. How we situate ourselves in space thru our senses— is extremely relevant and an important aspect of architecture. Increasingly we are living in a visually biased culture and our perception of reality is filtered exclusively through the visual. Architecture, on the other hand, has the capacity to expand our sensory repertoire; it can transform a condition to become immersive, sensual, and real.

DM: Where would you like to take these concerns next? What are the next issues to tackle?

MW: The constraints that defy easy categorization continue to fascinate us. The catalytic capacity of these constraints to form a distinct and specific language for a project keeps the nature of our work, by definition, agile and flexible. You know that we have long been dissatisfied with the seemingly reductive and inflexible nature of a traditional practice, constrained by the administrative boundaries of disciplinary distinctions. Projects that intrigue us are precisely those that avoid neat definitions, residing at the interstices between architecture, infrastructure, landscape architecture, and art. Our practice is biased toward a direct cut in section across disciplines, where a more synthetic and opportunistic approach informs the conceptual armature of each project. You might say

that the periphery of the traditional discipline of architecture will continue to inform the center of our practice.

MM: It's worth adding that we have discovered, in retrospect, that whenever we think we've established a clear plan for what we think we should be doing we have been thankfully derailed by the unexpected question, the unanswered provocation that has blindsided us and propelled us in surprising, productive, and new directions.

SMITH COL
CAMPU

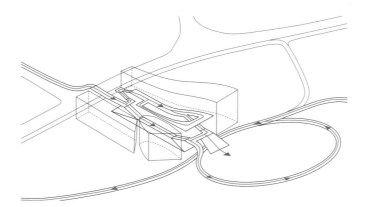

SMITH COLLEGE CAMPUS CENTER
NORTHAMPTON, MASSACHUSETTS

Students at Smith College–the largest liberal arts institution for women in the country–are assigned to houses, many of them Victorian-era structures complete with living rooms. Meant to foster a collegial environment, while successful, they also create isolated communities. Broadening the opportunity for social interaction, the Smith College Campus Center serves as a mediating body, the only building at Smith available to all students, faculty, and staff.

Serving as a junction between residential spaces and academic buildings, the sixty thousand-square-foot campus center is imagined as an elaboration of an en-route passage through campus. Defined by the interconnecting contours of frequently traveled pathways into and out of the college and constricted on two sides by existing structures, the building is oriented as a pathway: one end opening toward the community of Northampton, Massachusetts and the other onto the campus. The design clarifies Chapin Lawn, an expansive oval feature of Frederick Law Olmsted's original site plan that was never fully realized. By redefining this important element, the center establishes a prominent new setting for the 136-year-old school's historic structures.

The longitudinal expanse of the building's exterior is clad in a white-stained wood panel system reminiscent of board-and-batten construction and akin to the white clapboard construction of many Northampton buildings. Articulated by a seemingly random sequence of battens, the wood cladding activates the planar surface and weatherproofs the building with an innovative rainscreen assembly comprised of wood, plywood, steel, and insulation. The small apertures facing Elm Street, which faces the town, are subtle inclusions within a subdued facade, while the bold and expansive glazing on the campus side opens onto terraced steps that lead to Chapin Lawn. The broad steps provide the college with a central location for honorific events, including commencement ceremonies.

Inside, the lounges, exhibition areas, performance and dining facilities, student offices, mailrooms, and bookstore converge at a long atrium gallery, where light from above penetrates through the three levels to activate the core of the building. Expansive stairways open sightlines vertically throughout the interior and a bold color palette accentuates walls, carpeting, and custom furniture designed by Weiss/Manfredi.

Easily adaptable to different configurations, the furniture encourages occupants to inhabit and take ownership of the building. Throughout the atrium and in the dining hall, two related sets of café tables populate the space. A fragment of a highly chromatic botanical image printed on acetate is suspended within the cast-resin tabletops; when arranged together, the tables complete the botanical image. In the student lounge and throughout the building, lounge chairs offer restful places for reading or conversation; each is created from a single sheet of bent aluminum that allows the chairs to be gently rocked.

With its welcoming furniture and pathway orientation, the campus center closes the physical and social gap between residential and institutional buildings, creating a communal living room for the college.

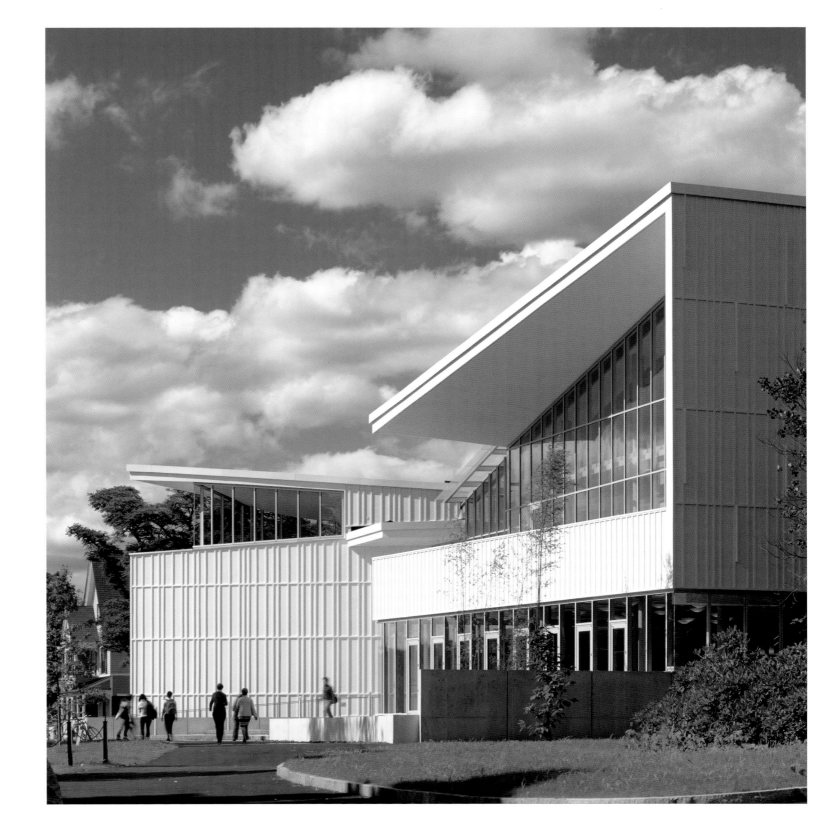

The configuration of the campus center mediates between the finely scaled town streets (Elm Street) and the campus where it expands to frame a newly defined oval. The serpentine gallery links all major program elements both planimetrically and sectionally.

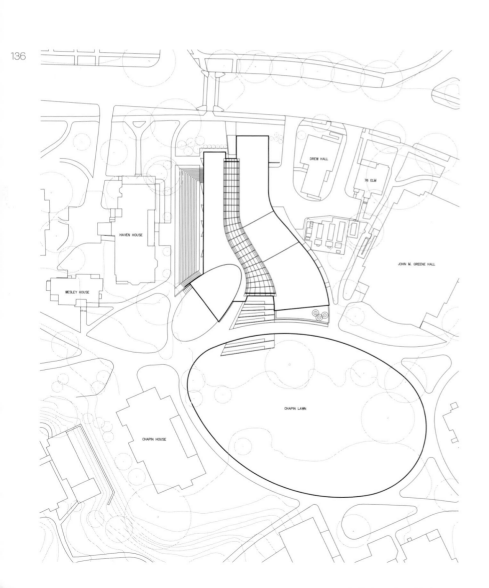

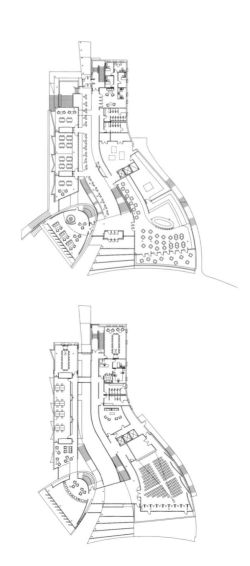

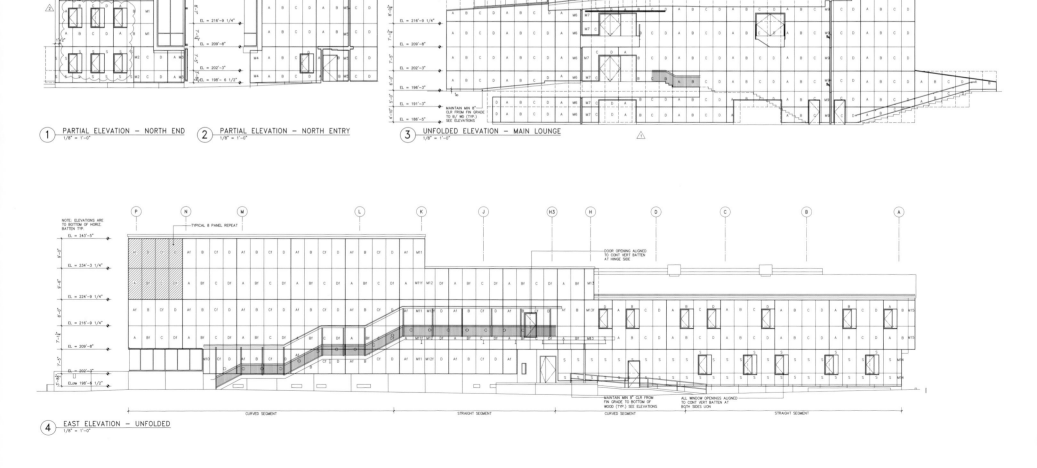

140

1 PARTIAL ELEVATION – NORTH END
1/8" = 1'-0"

2 PARTIAL ELEVATION – NORTH ENTRY
1/8" = 1'-0"

3 UNFOLDED ELEVATION – MAIN LOUNGE
1/8" = 1'-0"

4 EAST ELEVATION – UNFOLDED
1/8" = 1'-0"

NOTE: ELEVATIONS ARE TO BOTTOM OF HORIZ. BATTEN TYP.

MAINTAIN MIN 8" CLR FROM T/ ROOF TO B/ WD

MAINTAIN MIN 8" CLR FROM FIN GRADE TO B/ WD (TYP.) SEE ELEVATIONS

EL = 225'-4 1/4"
EL = 216'-9 1/4"
EL = 209'-8"
EL = 202'-3"
EL = 198'-6 1/2"

EL = 224'-9 1/2"
EL = 216'-9 1/4"
EL = 209'-8"
EL = 202'-3"
EL = 196'-3"
EL = 191'-3"
EL = 186'-5"

TYPICAL 8 PANEL REPEAT

DOOR OPENING ALIGNED TO CONT VERT BATTEN AT HINGE SIDE

EL = 243'-5"
EL = 234'-3 1/4"
EL = 224'-9 1/4"
EL = 216'-9 1/4"
EL = 209'-8"
EL = 202'-3"
EL = 198'-6 1/2"

MAINTAIN MIN 8" CLR FROM FIN GRADE TO BOTTOM OF WOOD (TYP.) SEE ELEVATIONS

ALL WINDOW OPENINGS ALIGNED TO CONT VERT BATTEN AT BOTH SIDES UON

CURVED SEGMENT   STRAIGHT SEGMENT   CURVED SEGMENT   STRAIGHT SEGMENT

The exterior rainscreen facade is comprised
of a system of pre-engineered wood panels.
A syncopated pattern of thin vertical battens
subverts the registration of the underlying
four-by-eight-feet modules and accommodates the shifting geometries of the plan.

144

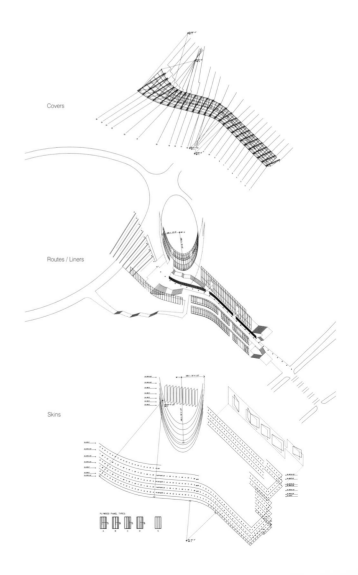

Covers

Routes / Liners

Skins

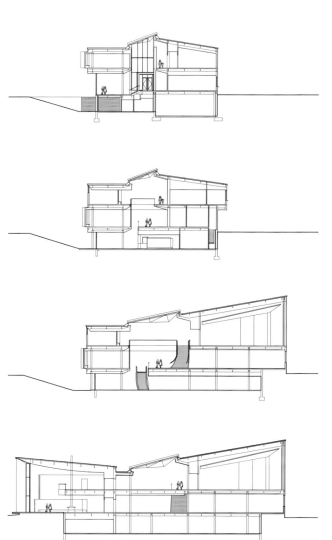

Custom resin tables are cast with magnified and manipulated images from Smith College's botanical collection. Sunlight from the skylight above projects tinted shadows onto the concrete floor.

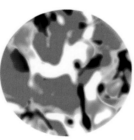

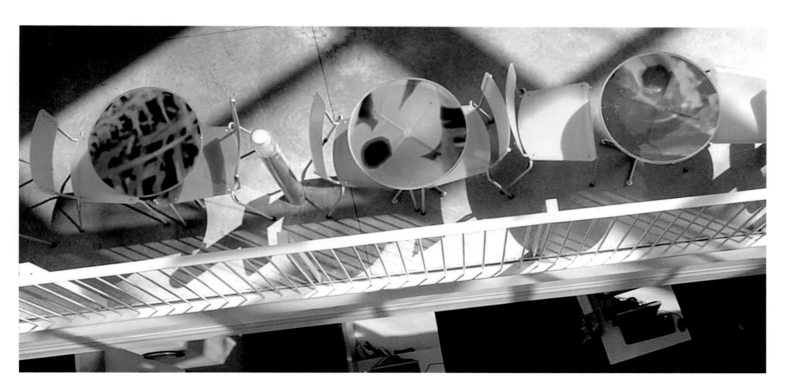

ROBIN HOO

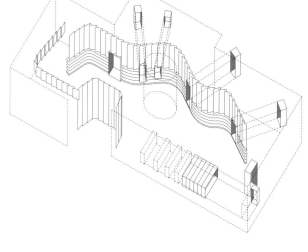

ROBIN HOOD LIBRARY
PUBLIC SCHOOL 42, ARVERNE, NEW YORK

New York City public schools in impoverished neighborhoods have rarely been able to afford or sustain properly equipped libraries. Reading levels at these schools have remained substantially below city averages. These facts captured the attention of both the New York City Department of Education and the Robin Hood Foundation, a nonprofit organization that leverages private funds to address poverty's root causes through a broad range of prevention programs.

The foundation's L!brary Initiative, launched in partnership with the Department of Education in 2001, aims to reverse "patterns of low literacy skills and underachievement by working with community school districts and public elementary schools to design, build, equip, and staff new elementary school libraries." The initiative has grown from a ten-school pilot program, each designed by a local architect on a pro-bono basis, to a group of more than fifty projects citywide.

One of the original ten, Public School 42 in Arverne, Queens, a five-story prewar brick edifice, had a small library in a converted fourth-floor classroom. Physically and visually isolated from the core of the elementary school's activities, the library was relocated to the ground floor, where it replaced one of two gymnasiums. The relocation gives the library a more central role in the school's daily rhythms. The design aspires to make the act of reading visually evident in a setting where learning and play are literally and philosophically connected.

The library's curvilinear wall affirms its unique status within the school; its variously sized inhabitable windows operate like the cutouts in a construction fence, providing selected views from the ground-floor hallway and cafeteria. Inside the library, a winding wood-paneled wall, conceived as a "book worm," holds volumes and reading alcoves. Adjustments to the space's geometry are made legible in the registration of scalar devices, such as the overlapping of flat panels to produce curved surfaces that provide a tactile and visual acknowledgment of the assembly sequence.

The architectural intent, playful and engaging, is also palpable in the library's moving parts. A deployable white theater scrim, suspended on a circular track and printed with text to resemble a crossword puzzle, provides the impression of privacy for reading groups while remaining transparent enough for librarians to supervise the activities. For school events, the rolling bookcases can be moved to one side of the library to create a large central space for group activities. Custom-designed rolling beanbag seats, student chairs, and other furniture can be arranged in a variety of informal settings.

With its inventively detailed prosaic materials (plywood, Plexiglas, and industrial carpeting), varied lighting, broad windows, and multiple computer stations, the library is a place that encourages learning and social interaction. The success of the project can be measured in its use: expanded hours, including Saturdays and evenings, were instituted not long after the new library opened its doors, to accommodate the school's popular family and community programming.

Formerly a gymnasium, the library includes a new perimeter wall that wanders among existing columns, creating study niches, reading alcoves, and maximizing the display of books.

Deployable furniture supports multiple
configurations for learning. A moveable
theater scrim with random texts
designed by Pentagram provides
an intimate and flexible reading area
within the main library space.

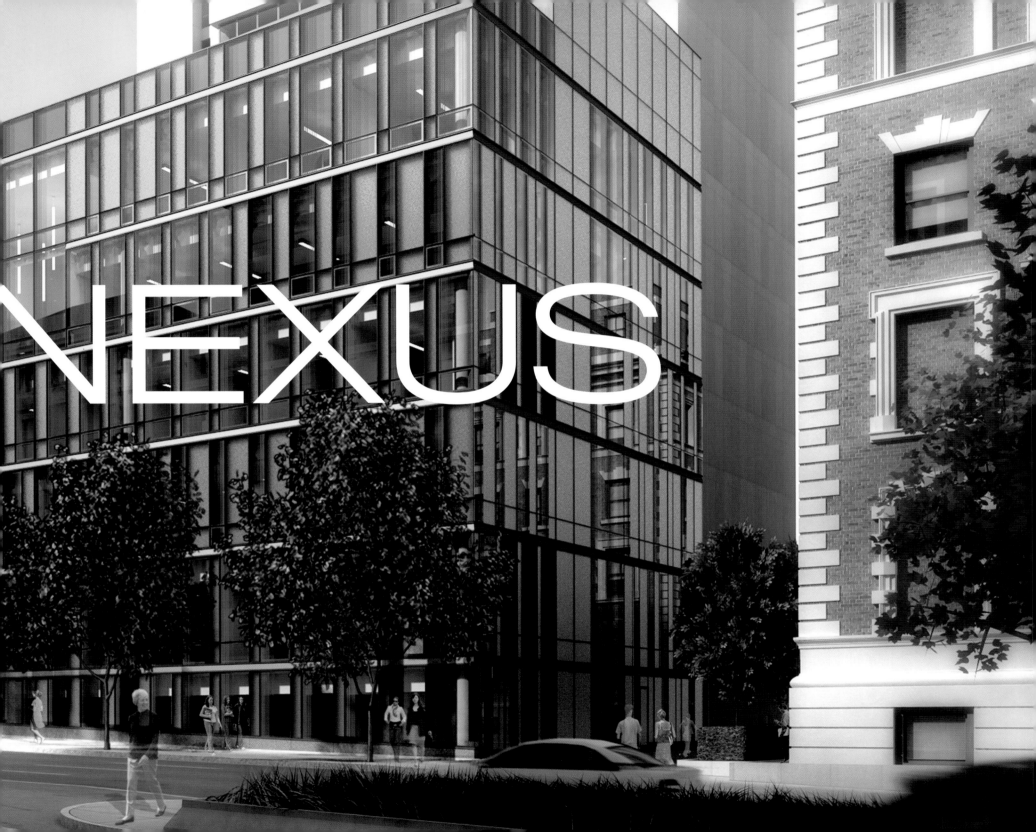

BARNARD NEXUS
NEW YORK, NEW YORK

Founded in 1889 as a women's college affiliated with Columbia University, Barnard College is an intimate campus compressed within the dense urban environment of Manhattan. Its academic program was originally located in Milbank Hall, a U-shaped beaux-arts edifice with a central courtyard that set a precedent for mixed-use buildings throughout the campus. Comprising an eclectic group of mostly brick buildings and defined by a series of disconnected landscaped spaces, today Barnard's campus is focused around Lehman Lawn, which is isolated from the historic Milbank courtyard by a fourteen-foot-high retaining wall and a plaza.

The Nexus, an 110,000-square-foot multi-use building, replaces a 1960s structure and establishes a new center for artistic, social, and intellectual life at the college. Located between Lehman Lawn and Broadway, the heavily glazed structure creates reciprocal relationships between landscape and architecture, interior and exterior, presenting a "window" onto the college and the city.

Focused on creating connections across the campus and throughout its various programs, Nexus links the historic and contemporary portions of the college through a series of grass terraces. The wedge-shaped design extends Lehman Lawn horizontally and vertically: descending planted terraces run north to Milbank Hall and ascending double-height atria bring natural light into the core of the seven-story structure. Carving a diagonal void through the building, the slipped atria create views to and through diverse program spaces and visually connect the lawn to the upper floors of the building and the vegetated, inhabitable rooftop.

Rethinking the often banal mixed-use building type, with its programmatically segregated spaces, Nexus brings together the college's currently dispersed programs of architecture, visual arts, dance, and theater by setting up visual juxtapositions that invite collaboration between disciplines. Continuous sightlines stretch through architecture, visual arts critique spaces, the library, and café, bringing together previously disconnected programs and constituencies.

Often difficult to achieve in multistory buildings, peripheral views are necessary to encourage cross-disciplinary dialogue. On the campus side of the building, a glazed, intentionally inefficient staircase encourages the informal encounters at the heart of a rich intellectual community and provides views to the surrounding campus. On the Broadway side, the atria establish unobstructed sightlines from the top floor of the building to Lehman Lawn and ensure that occupants are always aware of diverse and concurrent activities in the building.

The reciprocal relationship between landscape and program, which defines the organization of Nexus, is echoed in the reciprocity its envelope creates between the character of the campus and the diverse program elements of the building. Squarely centered in a campus defined by brick and terra-cotta, Nexus translates the static opacity of masonry into a luminous, integrally colored, and insulated energy-efficient skin. Panels modified with a translucent frit pattern mediate between solid and clear panels. Gradients of color, opacity, and transparency are calibrated to the Nexus's diverse program, allowing views into the building where they are appropriate and limiting visibility where programming requires privacy. The recombination of eight glass types produces an almost infinite variety of gradations.

Working in unison with the double-height slipped atria, visually expressed on Broadway, and the ascending stairs on the campus side, the building envelope reveals Barnard's vital mix of social, cultural, and academic programs.

Interior vistas through the slipped atria
provide connections between the cultural,
intellectual, and social spaces of the
Nexus. Vertically patterned glass marks
the primary circulation routes.

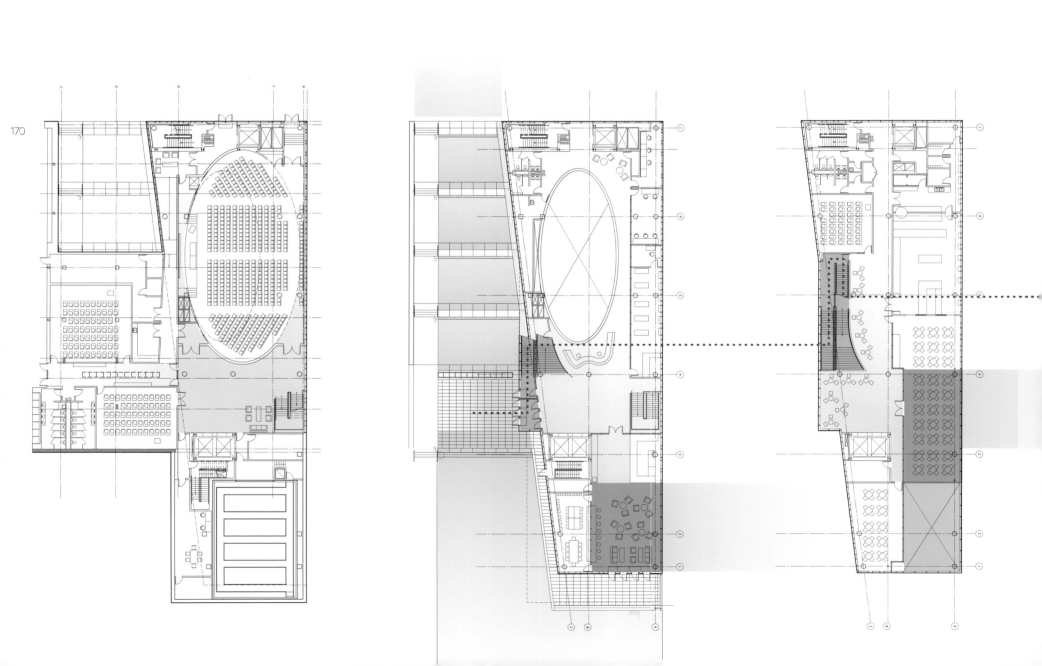

The diverse programs of the Nexus
open to the light-filled atria on the Broadway
side and are connected via a series of
ascending public stairs on the campus side
of the building.

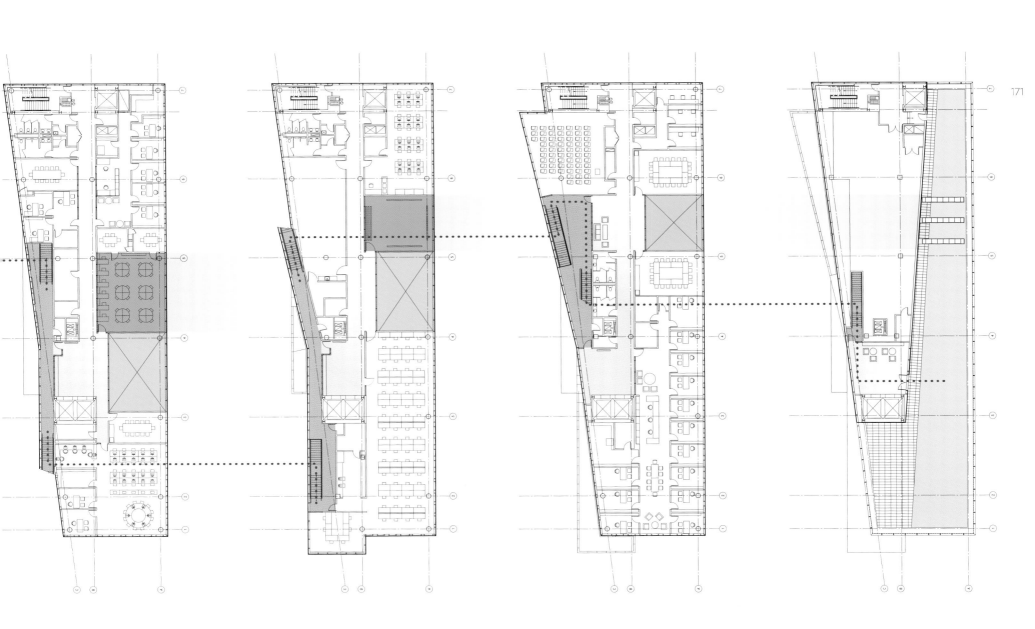

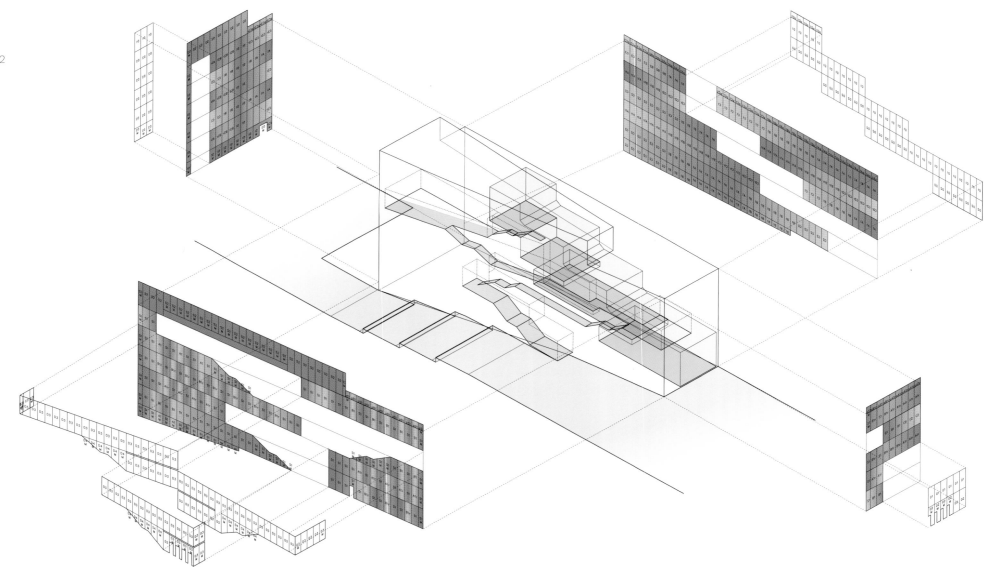

The chroma of the exterior glazing is carefully calibrated to complement the material qualities of the historic buildings at Barnard College. The translucent-colored glass shadow boxes create luminous planes within the building facade. Seven different window types provide infinite variations to accommodate a range of interior requirements.

EART

SKY

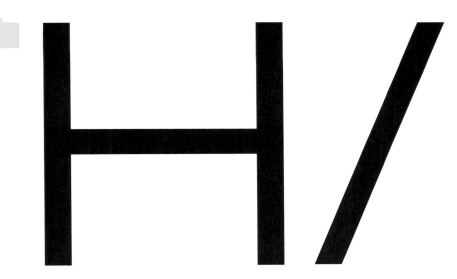

EPILOGUE
EARTH/SKY

The empty ground, our field's tabula rasa, has retained enormous currency since Le Corbusier declared piloti as the vehicle to liberate architecture from the heaviness of the earth. Rising above the ground allowed architecture to demonstrate, literally and philosophically, its elevated status. Ground became the required foil to the more heroic and exceptional status of architecture. Today, this position has ossified into a distorted imperative, evident in a profusion of forms in search of attention.

By contrast, the vast web of infrastructural systems that operate both above and below ground have often stood separately from the territory of architectural design, though the infinite nature of the horizontal terrain offers seemingly unlimited and subtle possibilities. Our own preoccupations reside in a broader definition of the cultivated landscape, incorporating the temporal characteristics of light and weather with the systemic logics of roadways, train lines, and storm-water networks. We're interested in harnessing the perceptual preoccupations of contemporary art, where material and surface expression can defy our preconceptions of what we see and experience, and in leveraging forces that extend beyond the boundaries of a site.

Operating outside the heroic language of architecture as immutable object, we leverage the forces of these temporal conditions, seen and unseen, to propose new potentials between surface and subsurface. When Le Corbusier articulated the distinction between object and ground, he relied on the production of otherness to establish architectural legitimacy. We prefer the possibility of

charging the intermediate space between ground and sky, implicitly questioning the fixed distinctions between both extremes. Put another way, our interest resides in developing a more gradated registration between material presence and immaterial phenomena, favoring reciprocal relationships between object and ground, surface expression and subsurface conditions.

We have focused our investigations on aspects of a project's cultural and physical characteristics that, prior to the imposition of new programs, remained unnoticed and untapped. At the same time, our intention is to establish constructive logics and material assemblies that resonate with each project and make those conditions visible. This essay, Earth/Sky, is a set of observations on the material realization of subsurface conditions, both physical and metaphorical, as well as the registration of the more temporal presence of light, sound, and touch.

At the Olympic Sculpture Park in Seattle, Washington we were interested in the interconnective potential between the layers of city, roadways, lighting networks, and train lines, creating a new stratum to link these distinctly separate systems. Originally three separate parcels, the sites could have been connected by two sculptural bridges or covered entirely with a comprehensive concrete lid. Instead, we opted for a continuous ribbon, an unfolding ground plane connecting the city to the water's edge. This strategy registered two explicitly different surfaces: a slow paced route across the site—visually connected with the horizon beyond—and the accelerated urban surface of cars, trucks, trains,

and trolleys. Tethered between the city and the elevated pathway, the topography alternately reveals or conceals the artifice of this new nature.

This hybrid approach informed material assemblies at the Museum of the Earth in Ithaca, New York. There, multiple berms are edged and stabilized by a new stratum of overlapping slabs of locally quarried sedimentary rock. Randomly sized slabs of the same stone, set in compacted gravel beds, define the terraced channel that collects rainwater runoff from the berms. In both conditions, the stone was split (not cut) parallel to its horizontal grain, revealing fossils imbedded in the rocks' layers and, in turn, the life-forms that were indigenous to the area millions of years ago. Thus, the construction performs an explicit pedagogical role while simultaneously meeting the technical demands of gravity, lateral loads, and channeling water through the museum site.

Similarly, in Seattle, the need to cap the contaminated site, which involved the placement of layers of highly compacted and engineered soils, supported our desire to develop an artificial topography. This new topography is given measure and scale through the precast concrete retaining walls that structure the site. The module of stepped overlapping panels creates an agile assembly, anticipating the adjustments of shifting and settling in this seismically live area. Diagonal geometries and stepped horizontals, rather than orthogonal alignments, create a forgiving framework—the repeating module of the panel system establishes a consistent meter.

This repetition of surface module also orchestrates a series of material effects. In the Barnard Nexus, a syncopated pattern of etched, colored, and translucent glass translates the chroma of the brick campus into a luminous terra-cotta colored surface. Tactile and soft, the acid etching of the exterior surface, modulated by a shifting gradient of transparency, translucence, and opacity, inverts the expectation of glass as clear and neutral and instead exploits its strong material presence.

At Smith College, the module of flat to hyper-extended battens on the surface of the campus center simultaneously secures the continuous wood surface to the substructure and distinguishes the four orientations of the building. Flat and evenly spaced battens mark surfaces in north or indirect light, and a syncopated module of extended and shallow battens on the curving south and east surfaces register the shifting geometry of the building through the changing depth of shadows as the sun wanders across the site.

Light, climate, sound, and movement produce a constant and invisible rhythm. Better understood by video artists and filmmakers, this quality is rarely exploited by architects. As such, the temporal becomes an active participant in the material development of our projects. In Seattle, the stepped concrete panels capture the projected colors of Teresita Fernandez's glass panels and register the time of year and orientation by the length of shadows at each interval. The stainless-steel panels on the street side of the park pavilion, pleated in strategic intervals, refract and reflect the Northwest's ever-changing weather patterns and the beams from passing car lights. Underfoot, the crushed stone walkway registers a change in sound as it moves from the surface of compacted earth, to the hollow surface of the bridge, to the ever shifting sand at the shore.

Ultimately we are interested in these unlimited possibilities. The continuous systems that extend beyond the project boundaries and the registration of temporal conditions together exploit the collaborative potential between surface and subsurface and activate the project of architecture.

At the Museum of the Earth, sculpted
parking berms, water terraces, and
a detention basin shape the site. Runoff
from the parking lot is first collected and
cleansed of petrochemicals in a series
of bioswales, then directed in descending
water terraces before being channeled into
a landscaped water detention pond. This
natural filtration process allows the water
to be released back into Lake Cayuga.

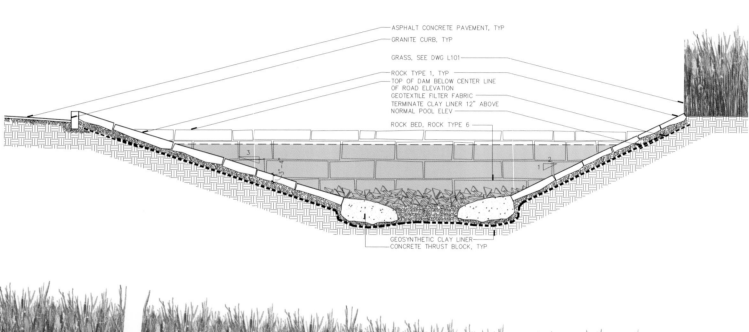

ASPHALT CONCRETE PAVEMENT, TYP
GRANITE CURB, TYP
GRASS, SEE DWG L101
ROCK TYPE 1, TYP
TOP OF DAM BELOW CENTER LINE
OF ROAD ELEVATION
GEOTEXTILE FILTER FABRIC
TERMINATE CLAY LINER 12" ABOVE
NORMAL POOL ELEV
ROCK BED, ROCK TYPE 6

GEOSYNTHETIC CLAY LINER
CONCRETE THRUST BLOCK, TYP

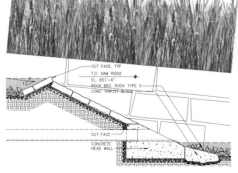

CUT FACE, TYP
T.O. DAM RIDGE
EL. 851'-6"
ROCK BED, ROCK TYPE 3
CONC THRUST BLOCK

CUT FACE

CONCRETE
HEAD WALL

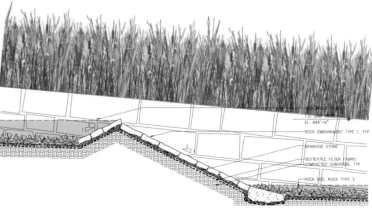

EL. 846'-6"
ROCK EMBANKMENT 1, TYP
DRAINAGE STONE
GEOTEXTILE FILTER FABRIC
COMPACTED SUBGRADE, TYP
ROCK BED, ROCK TYPE 3

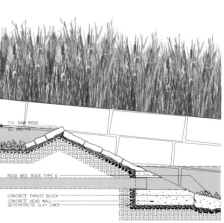

T.O. DAM RIDGE
EL. 842'-6"

ROCK BED, ROCK TYPE 6

CONCRETE THRUST BLOCK
CONCRETE HEAD WALL
GEOSYNTHETIC CLAY LINER

The shoreline for the Olympic Sculpture Park includes a newly created beach cove that allows direct access to the water's edge. The ten-foot tidal fluctuations provide a changing configuration in plan and section. Driftwood logs give scale to the arc of the beach and the terraced underwater environment encourages new salmon habitat.

183

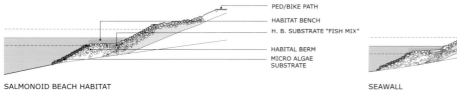

SALMONOID BEACH HABITAT

- PED/BIKE PATH
- HABITAT BENCH
- H. B. SUBSTRATE "FISH MIX"
- HABITAL BERM
- MICRO ALGAE SUBSTRATE

SEAWALL

- BEACH TERRACE
- INLET
- STORM DRAIN
- MONITORING WELL
- EXIST TIMBER PILES
- SEAWALL PILE

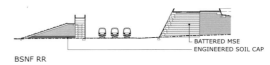

BSNF RR

- BATTERED MSE
- ENGINEERED SOIL CAP

184

As the Olympic Sculpture Park's Z-path landform descends from the pavilion to the water's edge its chameleon-like section reveals multiple roles: to elevate the pavilion, cross a highway, bridge over train tracks, connect to a new beach, and establish a series of salmon terraces.

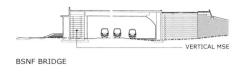

BSNF BRIDGE

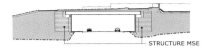

ELLIOTT AVE BRIDGE

ELLIOTT AVE

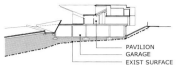

PAVILION

The forty-foot change in topography for the Olympic Sculpture Park was created with a mechanically stabilized earth system. Stacked steel baskets hold rock and gravel in place and are anchored by alternating layers of engineered plastic sheets and highly compacted soil.

A series of custom precast concrete panels protect the exposed mechanically stabilized earth construction and simultaneously create a guardrail where required. The slipped construction of the precast panels allows for controlled movement during seismic events. The tipped panels cast legible shadows that meter the scale of the retaining walls and become surfaces to receive projected images.

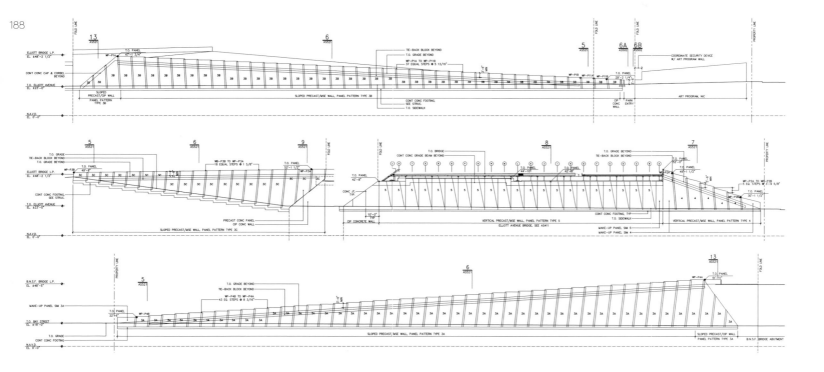

Throughout the park the cast-in-place concrete and precast panels alternate with strategically placed layers of steel mesh and layers of steel and glass. Retaining walls modify the topography where grades are steep and create intimate terraced settings for sculpture.

The skies of Seattle are active and changing. By night, the dampness in the atmosphere and the vitality of Seattle's urban setting create a range of light effects. The precast retaining wall softly reflects the glow of nighttime traffic, whereas the pavilion's stainless-steel folds distort and magnify ephemeral light conditions.

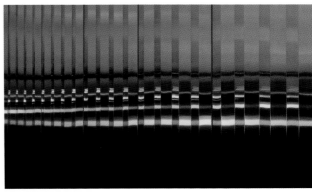

The urban setting of the pavilion is captured by a system of fritted mirrored glass, which reflects the changing street life both by day and night. Glass and stainless-steel panels register the pavilion's folded geometries.

STUDIO

Occupying the top floor of a former warehouse and factory building, the studio is illuminated by a skylight and has oblique views of the Empire State Building to the north and rooftop water towers to the south. During the day, the street is defined by endless deliveries to neighboring businesses; at night, the studio lights form a phosphorescent horizon against the backdrop of surrounding buildings.

Often, the debris of research and production overtakes the studio floors and walls. Research on all subjects—material samples, mock-ups, study models, digital animations, and an endless amount of drawings—are the artifacts of our purposefully open ended design process. We count on our studio's collective curiosity and peripheral vision to find relationships among these artifacts of our simultaneous investigations.

On occasion the abandoned studies from one project stimulate investigations in another. The search for resonance is nonlinear and opportunistic. We are suspicious of methodologies that become "signature" modes of designing and instead prefer a more agile exchange between scales and media. The necessity of production provides an impetus for research, and often the unpredictable detour invites surprise and innovation.

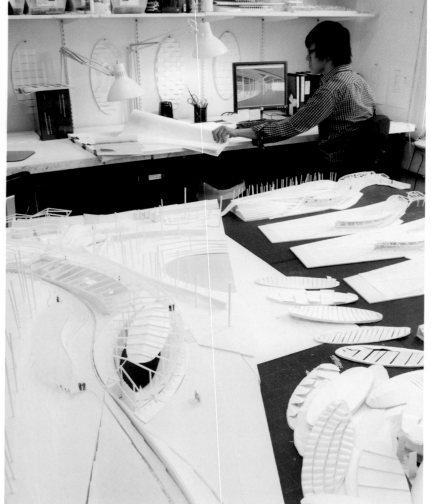

PROJECT CREDITS

Olympic Sculpture Park

Client: Seattle Art Museum

Weiss/Manfredi Team
Marion Weiss and Michael A. Manfredi (Design Partners), Christopher Ballentine (Project Manager); Todd Hoehn and Yehre Suh (Project Architects); Patrick Armacost, Michael Blasberg, Emily Clanahan, Beatrice Eleazar, Hamilton Hadden, Mike Harshman, Mustapha Jundi, John Peek, Aidi Su, and Akari Take-bayashi. Competition and Exhibition Team: Lauren Crahan, Kian Goh, Justin Kwok, Lee Lim, and Yehre Suh.

Consultant Team
Structural and Civil Engineering Consultant: Magnusson Klemencic Associates; Landscape Architecture Consultant: Charles Anderson Landscape Architecture; Mechanical and Electrical Engineering Consultant: ABACUS Engineered Systems; Lighting Design Consultant: Brandston Partnership Inc.; Geotechnical Engineering Consultant: Hart Crowser; Environmental Consultant: Aspect Consulting; Aquatic Engineering Consultant: Anchor Environmental; Graphics Consultant: Pentagram; Security and AV/IT Consultant: ARUP; Catering & Food Service Consultant: Bon Appetit; Kitchen Consultant: JLR Design; Retail Consultant: Doyle + Associates; Architectural Site Representation: Owens Richards Architects, pllc

Project Management: Barrientos LLC
General Contractor: Sellen Construction

NYC2012 Flushing Meadows Corona Park

Client: NYC 2012

Weiss/Manfredi Team
Marion Weiss and Michael A. Manfredi (Design Partners); Matt Azen, John Cooney, Jorge Filipe, Kian Goh, Christopher Payne, and Yehre Suh

Consultant Team
Landscape Architecture Consultant: Olin Partnership; Structural, Civil, and Traffic Engineering Consultant: Parsons Brinckerhoff Quade & Douglas, Inc; Ecology Consultant: Gaia Institute; Rowing Consultant: Mara Ford

Brooklyn Bridge Masterplan

Client: Lower Manhattan Development Corporation

Weiss/Manfredi Team
Marion Weiss and Michael A. Manfredi (Design Partners); Michael Harshman (Project Architect); Kian Goh, Amber Hong, Justin Kwok, and Na Sun

Consultant Team
Traffic Consultant: Parsons Brinckerhoff Quade & Douglas, Inc.; Structural and Civil Engineering Consultant: Weidlinger Associates Consulting Engineers; Lighting Design Consultant: Brandston Partnership Inc.; Security Consultant: Ducibella Venter & Santore; Pricing Consultant: Bovis Lend Lease

Museum of the Earth

Client: Paleontological Research Institution

Weiss/Manfredi Team
Marion Weiss and Michael A. Manfredi (Design Partners); Christopher Ballentine (Project Manager); Lauren Crahan and Armando Petruccelli (Project Architects); Michael Blasberg, Christopher Kimball, and Giselle Sperber

Consultant Team
Structural Engineering Consultant: Weidlinger Associates Consulting Engineers; MEPFP Engineering Consultant: MG Engineering P.C.; Civil Engineering Consultant: T.G. Miller, P.C.; Landscape/Horticulture Consultant: Elemental Landscapes; Lighting Design Consultant: Brandston Partnership Inc.; Exhibition Design Consultant: Weiss/Manfredi (Entry Hall) and Jeff Kennedy Associates (Exhibition Hall); Cost Estimator: AMIS Inc.

Owner's Representative: John Fontana, P.E.
General Contractor:
Hueber Breuer Construction Co., Inc.

Brooklyn Botanic Garden

Client: Brooklyn Botanic Garden

Weiss/Manfredi Team
Marion Weiss and Michael A. Manfredi (Design Partners); Armando Petruccelli (Project Architect); Christopher Ballentine, Michael Blasberg, Eleonora Flammini, Justin Kwok, Cheryl Maliszewski, Michael Steiner, Na Sun, and Rich Tong. Predesign team: Patrick Armacost, Kian Goh, and Michael Harshman.

Consultant Team
Structural and Civil Engineering Consultant: Weidlinger Associates Consulting Engineers; MEPFP Engineering Consultant: Jaros, Baum & Bolles Consulting Engineers; Geothermal/Geotechnical Engineering Consultant: Langan Engineering and Environmental Services; Landscape Architecture Consultant: HM White Site Architects; Lighting Design Consultant: Brandston Partnership Inc.; Cost Estimator: AMIS Inc.; Environmental Consultant: Viridian Energy & Environmental, LLC, Steven Winter Associates; Retail Consultant: Jeanne Giordano Ltd.; AV/Acoustics/Security Consultant: Cerami & Associates, Inc;

Security Consultant: TM Technology Partners; Food Service Consultant: Ricca Newmark Design; Curtain Wall Consultant: R.A. Heintges Architects Consultants; Traffic Consultant: Sam Schwartz LLC

International Retreat

Weiss/Manfredi Team
Marion Weiss and Michael A. Manfredi (Design Partners); Armando Petruccelli and Clifton Balch (Project Architects); Matt Azen, Chris Ballentine, Michael Blasberg, Hamilton Hadden, Todd Hoehn, Jessica Spiegel, Yehre Suh, and Akari Takebayashi. Predesign team: Kian Goh and Yehre Suh

Consultant Team
Structural Engineering Consultant: Weidlinger Associates Consulting Engineers; MEPFP Engineering Consultant: Jaros, Baum & Bolles Consulting Engineers; Civil Engineering Consultant: Dvirka and Bartilucci; Lighting Design Consultant: Brandston Partnership, Inc.; Curtain Wall Consultant: R.A. Heintges Architects Consultants; Landscape Consultants: Jim Stevenson and HM White Site Architects; Traffic Consultant: Dunn Engineering Associates; Cost Estimator: AMIS Inc.; Geotechnical Engineering Consultant: Park Engineering, P.C.; Food Service Consultant: Cini-Little International; AV/Acoustics/IT/Security Consultant: Shen Milsom & Wilke, Inc.; Fountain Consultant: CMS Collaborative; Fabrics Consultant: Lee Jofa; Gallery Curtain Consultant: Mary Bright Inc.; Furniture Consultant: BG Partnership

Owner's Representative:
Roslyn Consultants, LLC
Construction Manager:
Turner Construction Company

Smith College Campus Center

Client: Smith College

Weiss/Manfredi Team
Marion Weiss and Michael A. Manfredi (Design Partners); Tae-Young Yoon (Project Manager); Armando Petruccelli and Kian Goh (Project Architects); Michael Blasberg, Lauren Crahan, Stephanie Maignan, Chris Payne, Jason Ro, and Yehre Suh

Consultant Team
Structural Engineering Consultant: Weidlinger Associates Consulting Engineers; MEPFP Engineering Consultant: Jaros, Baum, and Bolles Consulting Engineers; Landscape Architecture Consultant: Towers|Golde Landscape Architects and Site Planners; Lighting Design Consultant: Renfro Design Group, Inc.; Civil Engineering Consultant: Fuss & O'Neill; Curtain Wall Consultant: R. A. Heintges Architects Consultants; AV/Acoustics/IT Consultant: Shen Milsom & Wilke; Security Consultant: Ducibella Venter & Santore; Food Service Consultant: Cini-Little International; Cost Estimator: AMIS Inc.; Waterproofing Consultant: James Gainfort

Construction Manager:
Daniel O'Connell's Sons

Robin Hood Library

Client: Robin Hood Foundation/ NYC Public School 42

Weiss/Manfredi Team
Marion Weiss and Michael A. Manfredi (Design Partners); Christopher Ballentine (Project Manager); Michael Blasberg, Chistopher Kimball, Jacquine Lorange, Stephanie Maignan, and Sara Stevens

Consultant Team
Lighting Design Consultant: Brandston Partnership Inc.; MEPFP Engineering Consultant: Louis Licameli, P. E.; Graphic Design Consultant: Pentagram

Construction Management:
Sciame Construction Co. Inc.
General Contractor: Volmar Services Inc.

Barnard Nexus

Client: Barnard College

Weiss/Manfredi Team
Marion Weiss and Michael A. Manfredi (Design Partners); Michael Harshman (Project Manager); Clifton Balch and Yehre Suh (Project Architects); Michael Blasberg, Hamilton Hadden, Patrick Hazari, Todd Hoehn, Anastasia Kostrominova, Justin Kwok, Lee Lim, Kim Nun, Nick Shipes, Michael Steiner. Predesign team: Patrick Armacost, Kian Goh, Jason Ro, Yehre Suh, and Tae-Young Yoon.

Client Team
MEPFP/Vertical Transportation Engineering Consultant: Jaros, Baum & Bolles Consulting Engineers; Structural Engineering Consultant: Severud Engineers; Civil Engineering Consultant: Langan Engineers; Curtain Wall Consultant: R.A. Heintges Architects Consultants; Lighting Design Consultant: Brandston Partnership Inc.; Landscape Architecture Consultants: HM White Site Architects; AV/IT/General Acoustics/ Security Consultants: Cerami & Associates, Inc., with T.M. Technology Partners, Inc.; Food Service Consultant: Ricca Newmark Design; Retail Consultant: Jeanne Giordano; Cost Estimator: AMIS Inc.; Sustainability Consultant: Steven Winter

Associates; Theatre Consultant: Fisher Dachs; Theatre Acoustic Consultant: Jaffe Holden Acoustics; Waterproofing Consultant: James Gainfort

Owner's Representatives:
Roland L. Ferrera and Patrick Maldoon
Construction Manager: Bovis Lend Lease

ACKNOWLEDGMENTS

Surface/Subsurface has presented an opportunity to reflect on the intertwining ideas, research, and projects that have informed the core of our thinking over the past decade. This effort has served as a forum to discuss an expanded idea of "content" with colleagues and collaborators; equal parts retroactive manifesto, open ended conversation, and a prologue to future action.

The work here reflects the collective talents and commitment of members of our studio who always test the limits of what we do. We are deeply grateful to project leaders who helped bring the work to reality: Christopher Ballentine, Armando Petrucelli, Yehre Suh, Mike Harshman, Todd Hoehn, Clif Balch, Lauren Crahan, Kian Goh, Tae-Young Yoon, and team members Patrick Armacost, Michael Blasberg, Justin Kwok, Patrick Hazari, Hamilton Hadden, Matt Azen, Mustapha Jundi, Lee Lim, Stephanie Maignan, Cheryl Maliszewski, Kimberly Nun, Jason Ro, Na Sun, Akari Takebayashi, Michael Steiner, Beatrice Eleazar, Emily Clanahan, John Peek, Christopher Kimball, Jessica Spiegel and Sara Stevens whose many contributions are evident in the work.

We are indebted to our clients: Mimi Gardner Gates, John Shirley, Chris Rogers, Richard Schaffer, Judith Shapiro, Liz Boylan, Lisa Gamsu, Ruth Simmons, Maureen Mahoney, Warren Allmon, Alex Garvin, Chris Glaisek, Scott Medbury, Patrick Collina, Ralph Morgan,